When Steamboats Reigned in Florida

UNIVERSITY PRESS OF FLORIDA

Florida A&M University, Tallahassee
Florida Atlantic University, Boca Raton
Florida Gulf Coast University, Ft. Myers
Florida International University, Miami
Florida State University, Tallahassee
New College of Florida, Sarasota
University of Central Florida, Orlando
University of Florida, Gainesville
University of North Florida, Jacksonville
University of South Florida, Tampa
University of West Florida, Pensacola

University Press of Florida

Gainesville / Tallahassee / Tampa / Boca Raton

Pensacola / Orlando / Miami / Jacksonville / Ft. Myers / Sarasota

When Steamboats Reigned in Florida

Bob Bass

Printed in the United States of America. This book is printed on Glatfelter Natures Book, a paper certified under the standards of the Forestry Stewardship Council (FSC). It is a recycled stock that contains 30 percent post-consumer waste and is acid-free.

13 12 11 10 09 08 6 5 4 3 2 1

Library of Congress Cataloging-in-Publication Data
Bass, Bob, 1938–
When steamboats reigned in Florida / Bob Bass.
p. cm.
Includes bibliographical references and index.
ISBN 978-0-8130-3235-1 (alk. paper)
1. Inland water transportation—Florida—History. 2. Steamboats—Florida—History. 3. Steam-navigation—Florida—History. 4. Florida—Description and travel. 5. Coastwise shipping—Florida—History. I. Title.
HE631.F6B37 2008 386.'22436—dc22
2008002686

The University Press of Florida is the scholarly publishing agency for the State University System of Florida, comprising Florida A&M University, Florida Atlantic University, Florida Gulf Coast University, Florida International University, Florida State University, New College of Florida, University of Central Florida, University of Florida, University of North Florida, University of South Florida, and University of West Florida.

University Press of Florida
15 Northwest 15th Street
Gainesville, FL 32611-2079
http://www.upf.com

The author and the publisher wish to thank
The Steamship Historical Society of America
for its generous contribution which
made this book possible.

Contents

1

A Brief History of Steamboats on Florida's Major Rivers

The people of our country have a rich history of travel. The inland waterways were the routes they used in our early days. These waterways include both the natural rivers and man-made canals that are found all over our country. Before the railroads the rivers were the natural arteries of travel. This is particularly true in Florida, which didn't have any railroads crossing the state until the late 1800s.

When Robert Fulton installed a steam engine in the side wheel boat *North River Steamboat* to drive the paddle wheels in 1807, a revolution in transportation took place. When steamboats were born, the world changed forever. The same type of steam engine that powered the *North River Steamboat* evolved to finally be used by railroads, and the world was changed again.

Fulton's steam engine was the marvel of its time. We will probably realize the impact of such an invention as the steam engine when modern cars and other vehicles are finally powered with something other than petroleum-based fuels.

As early as 1829, steamboats began to ply Florida's waterways, and these vessels were able to run upstream as well as down with relative ease. The new age of transportation had arrived. Goods that were once brought to settlers and pioneers by barge could now be replenished by the steamboats on a regular basis. The steamboats were colorful, raucous, dangerous, outrageous, and sometimes impractical in design. Along with the boats came the need to improve the waterways for easier and more dependable transportation.

Special dredges removed sand, sludge, and obstructions from the river bottom to keep the boats running and opened up sections of land that were once unnavigable. These special dredges did not appear until after the steamboat era on our Florida rivers. I mention them here only because they helped open up the waterways on some of the larger western rivers such as the Ohio, Mississippi, and Red River and were later used on our Florida rivers to improve navigation.

One such example of special dredges was the snag boat *Montgomery*. She was declared a National Historic Landmark in June of 1989 after serving on the Coosa and Alabama Rivers. In 1933, she was transferred to the Tombigbee and Warrior Rivers and her final days were spent on the Apalachicola, Chattahoochee, and Flint Rivers. The *Montgomery* was there until the boat was retired in 1982—at which time she was one of only two snag boats remaining in the United States. In 1984, the Mobile District of the Corps of Engineers awarded a contract for the complete restoration of the *Montgomery*. After her restoration, she was moored at the Tom Beville Visitor Center in Pickensville, Alabama, where the boat can be visited as a typical example of a snag boat (U.S. Army Corps of Engineers).

Even though steamboats revolutionized river travel, they were subject to hitting snags and obstructions in the rivers and many of them sank because of the hazards. Steamboats were a normal mode of travel by 1840, but most of them were lucky to survive five years of operation. Boiler explosions, fires, and sinking caused by obstructions in the rivers made steamboats markedly unsafe. Submerged trees, stumps, old boat wrecks, and sandbars blocked navigation and sometimes made it impossible to move. It wasn't until 1900 that the U.S. Army Corps of Engineers was given the responsibility for clearing the rivers, but the steamboat era in Florida was almost over by then.

Henry Millar Shreve was credited with designing the first steam-powered snag boat in 1829, and it was used on western rivers such as the Ohio, Mississippi, and Red in those early days. His first boat was called the *Heliopolis* and featured two hulls connected side-by-side that held a derrick to lift snags from the river. The double-hull design remained the standard until the twentieth century when steel hulls were fabricated. The only reason I mention snag boats is because they were severely needed in our Florida

Rivers. The work of clearing the way was done by the steamboat crews most of the time and sometimes by the passengers (U.S. Army Corps of Engineers, 2).

The economics of Florida towns like Palatka shifted from agricultural to tourism-based when steamboats came into common use. It seemed like everyone was riding them in the heyday. Sometimes Harriet Beecher Stowe could be seen waving from her front porch in her winter home in Mandarin on the St. Johns. General Robert E. Lee and General Ulysses S. Grant also used steamboats in their travels.

In April 1870, Robert E. Lee was persuaded to take a trip to the South because his health was not good at the time. It was hoped that the trip would improve his condition. He left for Florida from Lexington, Virginia, with his daughter and a Colonel Crowley of the British Army. The first part of their journey took them by train to Savannah, Georgia, where they spent the better part of two weeks. Great crowds of people met them everywhere they went, because Lee was the most famous and well-loved person of his time in the South. One purpose of his trip was to visit his father's grave at the Dungeness plantation in Cumberland Island, Georgia. General Henry "Light Horse" Lee died there on March 15, 1818, and was buried in the plantation cemetery. Robert E. Lee wistfully wrote his wife Mary, "I presume it is the last time I shall be able to pay to it tribute of my respect" (Mueller, *Steamboating*, 75). It was to be true since Lee died in October of 1870. After he left Dungeness, Lee boarded the steamboat *Nick King* in Savannah to depart for Florida. The *Nick King* certainly was not the best or newest vessel operating in the area for accommodating the Lee party, but it was probably made available gratuitously as was often the custom for distinguished passengers. The *Nick King* arrived in Jacksonville on April 13, 1870, and a large crowd of citizens assembled on the dock to witness the arrival and catch a glimpse of the man so honored and beloved by every Southern heart. Most of the crowd came aboard the steamboat and tried to shake hands with the general. It was noted that General Lee looked worn and feeble, but Lee indicated he was pleased with the journey and felt better since leaving Savannah. The *Nick King* left Jacksonville after only a thirty-minute stay and proceeded almost to Palatka, stopping at Orange Springs. The Lee party was to spend the night there at the home of Colonel Robert G. Cole, who had been the general's close friend and a member of his staff during the war. Unfortunately, the Cole home had burned about the turn of the century. The party had wanted to pick some oranges from Cole's grove, but it too had been destroyed. Finding nothing to keep them in Orange Springs, the Lee party departed again for Jacksonville. They arrived there at 4:00 p.m. and went to the home of J. P. Sanderson where a receiving line greeted the general. They also attended a party at the St. James Hotel. At 3:00 a.m. Lee's party departed for Savannah and thus ended what was destined to be the last time Lee ever saw Florida as he died at Lexington, Virginia, on October 12, 1870 (Mueller, *Steamboating,* 76–77).

General Grant's visit to Florida was under quite different circumstances from General Lee's. In fact, it was his first trip to the state. Grant, after finishing two terms as president, spent much time touring the United States and the world. Florida was the only state he had not visited. In 1880, he decided to visit Florida while on his way to Cuba.

Like Lee, Grant departed from Savannah, aboard the *City of Bridgeton.* He reached Fernandina on Sunday, January 4, 1880. At Fernandina, U.S. Senator David Yulee hosted a reception committee at the wharf. There was a formal affair in the evening consisting of a dinner and dance that was attended by many prominent citizens of the city.

The next day, Monday, January 5, the Fernandina City Fathers had a formal reception at City Hall. This was also well attended. General Phillip Sheridan, Mayor Brownson and Confederate General W. S. M. Davis occupied the platform with Grant, and Davis delivered the welcome speech. Davis declared that the people had accepted the results of the war, were loyal, and that Grant's visit would serve to further unite the country.

After the reception, the party got on the steamer *Florence* to visit the ruins of Dungeness on Cumberland Island. Grant wanted to visit the grave of General Harry Lee just as Lee had done ten years earlier.

Tuesday, January 6, Grant and his party boarded a special train to Jacksonville. Grant occupied a seat on the rear platform and indulged in smoking cigars and saluting the crowds of people who waved at him as the train slowly made its way to Jacksonville.

The next day, Wednesday, after a tour of the city, Grant boarded the mail steamer *Sappho,* which took the president on a sightseeing trip down and across the river to the Arlington area. Another banquet and ball was held in his honor at the Windsor Hotel.

On Thursday, January 8, Grant, Sheridan, and the rest of the entourage left Jacksonville for Enterprise on the steamboat *George R. Kelsey.* They spent the night at Palatka and were again honored with a ball.

The next day, Friday, the steamboat *Arrow* picked up the party to go to Enterprise. At Volusia Bar, due to low water, another steamer had to be engaged and the passengers transferred. After arriving at Enterprise the party spent the night at the Brock House. This famed hotel was the only one in the area suitable for a former U.S. president.

On Saturday, January 10, General Grant went to a ground-breaking ceremony in Sanford for the South Florida Railroad. He turned over the first spadeful of dirt for the new railroad.

On Sunday, January 11, Grant departed from Palatka on the steamboat *Osceola* for a sightseeing trip on the Okalawaha River. Everyone on the boat including Grant was delighted with the scenery and wildlife they observed while on the river.

On January 17, Grant visited Ocala and enjoyed a warm and hospitable reception even though there had been no advance preparation for his visit. On January 19, Grant and his party went to St. Augustine and then on to Jacksonville. The next day he left on a train for Cedar Key. There, the general boarded the steamboat *Admiral* and went to Cuba via Key West, where the party tarried for awhile.

Finally on January 22, the *Admiral* arrived in Havana and Grant's travels to and from Florida on a variety of steamboats was over (Mueller, *Steamboating*, 77–79).

In 1888, Jacksonville held Florida's first World's Fair called the Subtropical Exposition, and President Grover Cleveland attended. While President Cleveland was in Florida, he toured the area on a steamboat (Answers.com).

For around thirty years steamboating down the mighty St. Johns was an attraction for thousands of northern visitors—the first Florida tourists. The industry had begun. Hotels and restaurants sprang up everywhere along the routes that catered to these new visitors. Some of the larger boats were floating palaces that catered to every taste.

When the railroads finally came in the 1890s, the glamorous days of steamboating were over. They were enjoyed while they lasted by Floridians and visitors alike.

Although almost every river in Florida had steamboats plying their waters in the early 1800s, the major river systems had the most activity and more is known about them than about some of the minor streams.

The major rivers I write about in this book are the St. Johns, Ocklawaha, Kissimmee, Caloosahatchee, Apalachicola, and Suwannee. A lot of large and small rivers and lakes are also mentioned. They were on the route of the steamboats and significant in the development of travel on the waterways. The St. Johns and Ocklawaha rivers saw steamboat activity as early as 1829 that continued until 1842 during the Second Seminole Indian War when they were used to haul supplies for the troops engaged in the war. After the Seminole Wars, land grants were used as bounties for war veterans, inducing them to travel to and within the state, and steamboats offered most of the service. Land grants encouraged immigration, and by the 1850s, settlements were increasing on both coasts and particularly along the St. Johns.

During the Civil War the St. Johns was used by steamboats to transport goods and troops engaged in the war. One such steamer was the *Maple Leaf*. It was a luxury steamer that was pressed into service as a supply ship for the Union Army. The *Maple Leaf* was built in 1851 in Canada for carrying passengers. In 1862, she was sold to shipowners in Boston who chartered her to the Quartermaster Department of the U.S. Army for use as a transport. On April 1, 1864, the ship was carrying three infantry regiments on the St. Johns when she was sunk by a Confederate mine near Mandarin Point. She lay on the bottom until 1984 when she was rediscovered by divers of the St. Johns Archaeological Expedition led by Keith Holland (Maple Leaf Shipwreck). The rediscovery was to prove one of the most important in maritime history because the ship was so well preserved by the muddy river bottom. Among the relics discovered were large amounts of military goods as well as textiles, rubber, wooden musical instruments, and many other personal effects. Some of these could be identified with respect to the regiment, company, and sometimes the original owner.

Important documents that relate to the *Maple Leaf* have followed her since she was first built. Ship specifications such as the size of her hull and notes about the internal workings of her engines are good examples. Contemporary personal accounts, memoirs, and newspaper articles also provide important information. These documents have left a trail of history for the ship that is a very scarce resource in the study of maritime history and the War between the States. A number of things are known about the vessel—for example, she was the darling of the city of Rochester, New York, during her Lake Ontario days, a status that resulted in a vast amount of press coverage. The ship was once captured, in 1863, by Confederate prisoners who were on board. This event has been recorded by several of the participants. She was also the first steamboat to be blown up by a Confederate mine. More will be known after the salvage effort is complete and all the relics studied (Towart, 1–3).

The St. Johns River system was probably the most used and widely known system in Florida. Its history has been well recorded in the past, although most books on the subject are now out of print.

Passenger service began on the St. Johns and Apalachicola as early as 1829, and regular service was established on the St. Johns in the early 1830s to Savannah. In 1850, service was offered from Charleston, with Palatka being the normal head of navigation for the boats.

Prior to the steamboat activity on the St. Johns and Ocklawaha, the rivers were used for logging the highly valued lumber from surrounding forests. Cypress and cedar were plentiful, and great rafts of logs were floated down the Ocklawaha to the St. Johns and shipped by schooner to Jacksonville's saw mills (Mueller, *Ocklawaha*, 2).

There was also commercial barge traffic. Barge operations usually started at Palatka and ended at a point on the Ocklawaha that was determined by the depth of the water at the time and the demand for the goods transported by the barges.

These barges were powered by large groups of men who did the man-killing work of poling them on the river. Each man on the barge was given a long pole. He placed it in the water at the bow of the barge and walked to the stern pushing on the pole as he went. The work was laborious and time-consuming, but small settlements along the river were supplied with goods for several years from these barges (2).

No steamboat book about Florida would be complete without the story of Jacob Brock. He was born on July 5, 1810, and was one of fifteen children. His father was a leader in the Congregational Church and a river man himself at one time. Brock's family was from Vermont.

Not much is known about Jacob's early career in Hartford, Connecticut, except that he was once listed in a Hartford city directory as an engineer. We know he was also married and the father of four children while there. Sometime in 1840 Jacob left Connecticut and went to South Carolina, where he constructed the side-wheeler *Darlington,* no doubt named after the South Carolina city. He also added the title of captain to his name. The *Darlington* was to serve him well while he worked on the Pee Dee River hauling cotton and other goods. He spent three years on the Pee Dee, and then decided to move to Jacksonville, Florida, and try to start a business there. Jacksonville was already established as a seaport, with passengers and freight moving between Charleston, South Carolina, and Savannah, Georgia.

On the St. Johns River in Jacksonville, trade and passenger service was consistent between the port and the town of Palatka, Florida, but the river south of there was another story. It was not often traveled by steamboats because of unknown obstructions and unknown depths in the river. Brock decided to open up travel to the sleepy little town of Enterprise, Florida, which was on the eastern shore of Lake Monroe, and to travel farther south at a later time. He began by purchasing some land about a mile west of Old Enterprise, and he called his property New Enterprise. Here Brock laid out streets and lots and built a steamboat wharf. There was already a small store and boarding house on the property. In the fall of 1853, regular service to Enterprise was started with his steamboat, the *Darlington*.

Prior to this, Brock owned the steamboat *Sarah Spalding* and used her on the run to Palatka, but she suddenly disappeared and nothing was heard about her after 1853 (Mueller, *Steamboating*, 51–52).

Even though Jacob Brock was from the North, when the War between the States broke out, he sided with South and got in trouble helping some Confederates to escape from the Yankees. For this, he suffered many business and personal losses. The Yankees seized his steamboats and put him in prison. After the war, he was released and regained almost everything (Mueller, *Steamboating*, 54–55).

Brock's many accomplishments included starting a shipyard in Jacksonville that later became the famous Merrill Stevens yard of today. He also built a tugboat that towed in many a stranded steamboat. Jacob became the agent for a petroleum-derived lamp fuel to replace sperm whale oil that helped light up Florida homes. It was called kerosene.

Captain Jacob Brock died at age sixty-six on September 22, 1877. Ten years after his death, the St. Johns and Halifax Railroad reached Daytona, and the Jacksonville, Tampa, and Key West Railroad reached Sanford, where it connected with other railroads going south and west. The coming of the railroads slowed steamboat traffic on the St. Johns. That, along with other events of the time, signaled the end of the era (62). Between 1884 and 1885, the town of Enterprise went to sleep again. Today, all that is left is a road intersection and the Methodist Children's Home on the shore of Lake Monroe.

The Apalachicola River drainage covers almost 20,000 square miles, making it one of the largest river systems in the southeastern United States. The river and its tributaries drain most of eastern Alabama, west Georgia, and the Florida Panhandle. The river begins where the Chattahoochee and Flint come together in Lake Seminole near the Georgia-Florida state line.

Today, the system is navigable for a distance of 285 miles. The Apalachicola runs upriver to the Seminole Reservoir for 106 miles. The Chattahoochee goes a distance of 154 miles to Columbus, Georgia. The eastern arm of Lake Seminole meets the Flint River, which can be navigated to Bainbridge, Georgia, a distance of about twenty-five miles (Apalachicola and Chattahoochee Rivers).

Cotton from the plantations in Georgia was an important product in the 1800s and was sent down the Apalachicola by flatboats as early as 1822 to "Cotton Town." The name was changed to West Point in 1828 and finally incorporated as Apalachicola in 1831 when it became the county seat (Franklin County Local History).

The first steamboat to travel the Apalachicola was the *Fannie* (or *Fanny*), which was built in New York and brought to Florida through the coastal waterways in 1827. On January 28, 1828, she created a sensation as the first steam-powered vessel to arrive in Columbus, Georgia, through the Apalachicola and Chattahoochee river systems. Soon after that, schooners were arriving in Apalachicola to transport cotton and other goods brought downriver by steamboat to eastern American and European cities. This was also the beginning of passenger service from Florida all along the Apalachicola, Chattahoochee, and Flint River waterways (Mueller, *Perilous Journeys*, 16–17).

Most of the boats like the *Fanny* were designed for the deeper eastern rivers and had trouble navigating the shallow southern waterways, so they were replaced with boats that followed the design of Henry Miller Shreve of Ohio.

These boats were equipped with more powerful high-pressure engines and were built with double decks to accommodate passengers and cargo. Ohio River boat builders produced most of the boats that were used on the Apalachicola. In 1834, a boat named the *Hyperion* was built especially for the river and was delivered through New Orleans to Captain Adam Leonard of Apalachicola (Keeton and Kane)

The War between the States brought a flurry of activity from the steamboats, and much of it in Florida happened around Apalachicola Bay and the river. These were hard times for people in the rural South that turned much harsher during the war. Thousands of men left their families to fight, and these departures left all the work to their wives, the very young, and the old. It was more than some of them could do to get the crops planted and harvested as well as carry out the other chores that had to be done on the farms and plantations of the South. Those along the Apalachicola River faced another hardship—the Union blockade of Apalachicola Bay. At first, the blockade was inconsequential because the Union had so few ships to adequately patrol some 3,500 miles of Confederate coast from Virginia to Texas. Blockade runners were still able to move goods from the steamboats to the sailing ships and get them to their destinations.

Two months after the first shots were fired at Ft. Sumter, two ships appeared off Apalachicola Bay. These first ships were ill-equipped to deal with the Confederate vessels. They had deep hulls for stability at sea and were too big to navigate safely in the shallow waters. One hundred days after the arrival of the Union ships in the area, they captured their first quarry. On August 26, 1861, sailors lowered five small boats from the Union ships and headed into Apalachicola Bay. They captured the oceangoing vessel *Finland* and began preparing the ship for towing in the custody of the Union ships. After working all night in preparation, finally at dawn they began towing. But the sailors, unfamiliar with the area and battling unfavorable winds and current, beached the *Finland* on a sandbar only four miles from the safety of the Union ships. After frantically trying to free the ship, they noticed a steamboat towing an oceangoing vessel apparently into Apalachicola Bay. All at once, the steamboat switched directions and headed directly toward the *Finland.* On the deck of the steamboat were nine Confederate militia members armed with rifles. The sailors, knowing the water was too shallow for their ships to rescue them, set fire to the *Finland* and scrambled into their boats. By the time the Confederates arrived the *Finland* was engulfed in flames and very few items could be recovered from her (Exploring Florida).

The Suwannee River winds for almost 266 miles through swamps, high limestone banks, hammocks of hardwood, and salt marshes. The swamps also contained the much sought-after cypress trees that would become an important commodity along with cotton from plantations in the North. The Suwannee is a federally designated wild river and is the only major waterway in the southeastern United States that is still unspoiled and in some places much the same as it was years ago. There is even a white-water rapid at Big Shoals and Little Shoals located upstream from the town of White Springs (History for Fanning Springs State Park).

Although there was a lot of activity on the Suwannee in the early days, accounts are very sketchy about the details. The Suwannee and Apalachicola were two of the most traveled rivers of the 1880s, but somehow information about the Suwannee didn't get written down. People were so busy making a living in those days they thought it wasn't necessary. Some of the Suwannee River steamboat story is detailed here. More is covered in the last chapter of the book.

Paddle wheelers were used in the endless pursuit of the Indians during the Seminole Wars. When Fort Fannin was built, there was regular steamboat service between Fannin Springs and Cedar Key. The fort was originally called Palmetto but was renamed for Colonel Alexander Campbell Wilder Fannin. The colonel was born in 1788 and lived until 1846. He served under General Andrew Jackson during the Seminole Wars and was noted for his outstanding service during a battle near the Withlacoochee River where he was sent to capture Seminoles for deportation (Kaucher, 13).

Steamboat traffic on the Suwannee began in the winter of 1836 when a boat brought supplies to the fort at Suwannee Springs five miles below White Springs. The fort was crowded with soldiers as well as families of local settlers gathered there to escape the Indians. The fort was cut off from supplies because of extremely high water in the river. When the water started dropping in the winter of 1839, a steamer from the army base at Cedar Key went up the river bringing the much-needed supplies. The trip was very hazardous because of shoals in the river and shallow water in some places (12).

Another early boat was the steamer *Madison* that was operated by Captain James Tucker. He owned and ran the *Madison* and traveled the Suwannee carrying all sorts of goods to sell to the settlers along the river. The *Madison* carried cowhides, beef, tallow for candles, chickens, eggs, hogs, venison, beeswax, and a host of other goods. The boat wasn't large, but her whistle could be heard for miles as she traveled along the river, bringing the farmers, woodsmen, and planters to the landing with their goods to barter.

Captain Tucker was active in the Civil War and raised a company of Confederate soldiers that captured a federal gunboat in the Gulf of Mexico. They slipped out of the Suwannee during the night and caught the sleeping

Yankees near the mouth of the river. Later, Tucker and his company were assigned to Virginia where their mission was to deliver corn to the starving people. He left the steamboat behind to bring a load of corn to his neighbors. They and their animals were starving because there was no food. The agreement was to haul the corn from Suwannee Old Town near the mouth of the river and then sink the boat in Troy Springs so the Yankees could not use her. The priceless load of corn was brought upriver, and then at around two o'clock in the afternoon in September, 1863, the boat was taken to Troy Springs. The plugs were removed and the *Madison* sank to the bottom. Captain Tucker never returned to claim what was left. Sometime during the war the boat's boilers were removed and carried to the coast where they were used in the manufacture of salt. The remaining materials on the boat were used by the local residents. Only the hull remained, and it can sometimes be seen when the river is just right, still resting on the bottom (Carr).

Another event of the Civil War took place on the Suwannee at the Yulee Plantation near Madison, Florida. There the last followers of the Confederacy learned President Davis had been captured. They had left Charlotte, North Carolina, with a wagon train containing the last material remains of the Confederate States of America. They had hoped to make it to Texas and revive the government. They were traveling toward the West through the wilderness of the Suwannee Valley when they got the news about President Davis (Kaucher, 14).

Shortly after the war ended, in 1865, steamboats became numerous on the river. Captain R. A. Ivey built several boats in Branford and earned the city a name as a boatyard. His most famous boat was the *Belle of the Suwannee.* It was launched in December of 1889 to haul freight and passengers. The boat had several staterooms and gained fame as a paradise for honeymooners. One of the staterooms was designed as a bridal chamber. At the very height of her fame the *Belle* floundered at the mouth of the Steinhatchee River on September 29, 1896 (Burnett).

One of the largest of the Suwannee boats was the *Three States.* The boat was so long it was difficult for her to turn around, especially in the river above Branford. Her main purpose was hauling freight.

Mention should be made of Dan McQueen. He was a mulatto pilot who was born a slave in 1860 in Old Town, Florida. He began steamboating at age eleven as a dishwasher on the *Wawenock.* He worked for six years on the *David L. Yulee* for $3 a month and finally as its mate for $40 a month. It was said that he knew everything there was to know about the Suwannee. He knew every snag, sandbar, and alligator hole. Some say he even piloted the *Belle of the Suwannee* at one time. McQueen had a master's license and sometimes captained other boats when he wasn't operating his own. He served as a teacher in a black school in Old Town for a time (Florida's Underwater Archaeological Preserves).

During the brisk trade days of the 1880s and 1890s, a variety of boats plied the river. Most were flat-bottomed, shallow draft boats with double decks around 200 feet long. Like most early boats they were wood fired and depended on the fat lighter wood found in the woods around the river. Some carried passengers and had their accommodations on the top deck. All were smaller versions of the steamboats found on the Mississippi River. One such boat was the *Louisa*, built entirely for hauling freight. She was owned by Captain E. R. McGruder who once won a $100 bet by taking her to White Springs with a load of freight. Although McGruder won the bet, the repair cost for the trip was $3,000 because of all the hazards he

1. The steamboat *Louisa* on the Suwannee. Originally built as a freighter and later used to haul passengers. Photo used by permission of the Florida Photographic Archives.

encountered on the river. The *City of Hawkinsville* was the largest and the last steamboat to see service on the Suwannee. She was brought to the river in June 1900 to aid in the booming lumber industry. The boat was 141 feet long and built in Abbeville, Georgia, in 1886 originally for the Deepwater Boat Lines in Hawkinsville. She was sold to the Gulf Transportation Company of Tampa and belonged to them when she came to the Suwannee. Steamboat activity came to a halt on the Suwannee around 1922, and the *Hawkinsville* was abandoned just south of the railroad trestle in Old Town, Florida. Her remains can be visited today by divers in the river. The old boat rests in shallow water on the western bank of the river about 100 yards from the railroad trestle she helped build. The railroads were the end of the steamboat era here and all over Florida (Kaucher, 10–11).

The port of Cedar Key is approximately fifteen miles from the mouth of the Suwannee River in the Gulf of Mexico and accounted for a lot of the steamboat traffic on the river. Once a lively port and railhead, it is now a quaint fishing and tourist village. Cedar Key was supplied with cedar lumber to keep two local pencil manufacturing plants going and for shipping to northern pencil plants.

Passengers from the upper reaches of the Suwannee and a lot of other places along the coast came to Cedar Key to enjoy the fishing and seafood delights. Cedar Key was a very popular destination for tourists, writers, and speculators of all kinds. The lumber that was floated down the Suwannee in great rafts was pushed along by the steamboats all the way.

The *David L. Yulee* was built in 1875 and operated on the river between Cedar Key and Branford, 110 miles upriver from Cedar Key. The *Yulee* was of 89 tons and was 82 feet long by 22 feet wide with a draft of 4 feet. The boat was built in Cedar Key with a square stern and one deck.

Owners of the vessel were Captain John Gleason, and later, Samuel C. Redick. Redick was listed as master of record for most of the boat's life.

Branford, Florida, was known as a boat-building town in the days when the *David L. Yulee* served the community. The *Yulee* was abandoned in Plumer's Bend not far from the Gulf of Mexico in 1885 (Will, 42–43).

Other boats that served on the Suwannee were the *Thetis, Sam Pyles, C. D. Owens, Shepherd, Robert,* and *Annie M.* No data are available on these boats other than that they were on the river.

The Caloosahatchee was once called "Beautiful River" in the steamboat days when the river twisted and turned in every direction. There were fragrant-smelling orange groves around some of the bends along with oaks streaming with moss, cabbage palms, and cypress trees. Land salesmen from around Ft. Myers coined the name "Beautiful River" and said it was from a Seminole Indian word. The truth is, the river was named after the Calusa Indians who lived along the banks long before the Seminoles (47–48).

Hamilton Disston, in 1881, began dredging and draining the low-lying areas through Lake Hicpochee, Lake Flint, Lettuce Lake, and Bonnet Lake, making the waterway suitable for boat traffic to run all the way from Lake Okeechobee to Ft. Myers. Before all this could be done, a rock ledge that had created a waterfall in the river at Ft. Thompson had to be removed. This ledge held back a lot of the water coming from Lake Okeechobee. One of the old steamboat captains, Fred Menge, blasted out the ledge in 1881. When the ledge was removed, it created rapids that were a hazard to navigation until 1909 when the dredge *Caloosahatchee* cleaned out the run and made the river passable to almost any boat (30).

2. *Poinsettia* is moored beside the Duval warehouse on the Caloosahatchee River. After steamboats came to the Caloosahatchee, commerce and the lives of those along the river were vastly improved. Photo used by permission of the Florida Photographic Archives.

Towns along the river, such as Moore Haven and LaBelle, began to grow and prosper once the steamboats started their regular trips. Today, Moore Haven has the first lock in a flood control system that extends down the river to Ft. Myers. I once traveled aboard my houseboat along with three other boats from Lake Kissimmee to Ft. Myers and back. Moore Haven was our first stop. We spent three days there while the lock was being repaired. After we got through the lock, we stopped at LaBelle and spent another three days exploring the town and surrounding countryside. The trip was a memorable experience for me because I had been studying the steamboat era for some time, and here I was traveling on one of the steamboat rivers.

LaBelle was founded by Captain Francis Asbury Hendry who laid out the first streets. He was a Confederate captain in the War between the States and had discovered the Caloosahatchee during one of the Seminole Wars. Hendry had been raising cattle on the Alafia River and bought 30,000 acres of land around LaBelle, where he moved his cattle business. He bought herds from others and along with his own sold them to Cuba (Will, 47).

Everett E. Goodno bought a few thousand acres of land from Francis Hendry which included the township of LaBelle; there by the river, he built a hotel called the Everett Hotel. Land company boats taking prospects to Lake Okeechobee stopped there, and the town soon began to prosper with three stores and a blacksmith shop.

Ft. Thompson was a couple of miles from LaBelle and was the place where droves of cattle crossed the river on their way to Punta Rassa to be shipped to Cuba. In the steamboat days Ft. Thompson was probably the most important place on the upper river. Everett Goodno built an ice plant at Ft. Thompson that was making a lot of money when the catfish industry started on Lake Okeechobee and the steamboats were taking loads of fish to Ft. Myers (53).

Francis Hendry and another cattle baron, Jacob Summerlin, laid out the route for the canal from Ft. Thompson to Lake Hicpochee by hacking their way through the lakes and saw grass marshes and putting out flags for Disston dredges to follow. The dredges widened and deepened the canals so steamboat traffic could get through. Summerlin was sixty years old at the time, but he and Hendry knew the country better than anyone else. They laid out the canal at their own expense.

The last river to be discussed in our brief history is the Kissimmee. Since

3. Captain Bob Bass aboard the houseboat *Linda Gale*. Photo used from the Bass Photo Collection.

the third chapter in our book is exclusively about this river, a lot of details are omitted here and covered in that chapter. I will say that very little is recorded about steamboat activity on this river.

I have personally traveled the Kissimmee system for the last twenty years, and it is the river that started my interest in steamboats. I found out that I have an ancestor who was the first mayor of Kissimmee, Florida, and the first chief of police. His name was Thomas Alexander Bass, and he was my great-grandfather's brother. Among Tom Bass's achievements, he was a steamboat captain who owned several different boats during his lifetime. Another Thomas Bass is credited with starting the catfish business on Lake Okeechobee. I believe when one has a personal stake in the history of our great state, it becomes all the more interesting and meaningful. Tom Bass started my research and I will be eternally grateful. He also started me on the way to being a writer.

Much of the time I have spent on the river has been aboard my houseboat *Linda Gale*. The boat is 40 feet long and has a beam of 12 feet, just about the size of many of the steamboats that traveled the Kissimmee. When I am aboard my boat, I can almost visualize the river as it was in the steamboat days and imagine myself captain of one of the steamers. The boats were all shallow draft vessels and utilized pine lighter wood for fuel most of the time. The fuel had to be collected at the various stops along the river; it was cut by the local pioneers or settlers in the area and stacked at the steamboat landings. This practice was common all over Florida in the early days. The boats that used this fuel were called smoke boats because of the large amount of black smoke that came from the stacks. Wood was especially plentiful in the pine forests along the Kissimmee. The pine sap that came from the pine trees was also used by early naval boatyards as pitch to seal the seams in oceangoing vessels. I am sure it was also used in a lot of steamboats for the same purpose.

Another trait of the Kissimmee River boats was the name coined in the area for them. They were called "wet tail" steamboats because of the constant shower of water that fell on the stern of the boat while it was under way. Although there were some side-wheelers, the majority of the Kissimmee boats were the wet tail variety. The paddle wheel was in the very aft part of the boat because of the tight curvature of the Kissimmee River that was sometimes described as looking like a serpent's back. It twisted and turned so much that a boat could be seen heading in one direction one minute and then another in the next. The Kissimmee and the Ocklawaha were a lot alike in the way they twisted and turned, and the boats that traveled these rivers were very similar in design. In the early days fallen trees and other obstructions had to be cleared by the steamboat men themselves. There was no Corps of Engineers on the rivers as there is today.

The river was full of overhanging branches and vines that sometimes had to be cut before a steamer could proceed on the journey. Water hyacinths were a big problem that had to be cleared on some stretches of the river. The aft paddle wheel helped in these situations.

As civilization advances, change comes to all the rivers the steamboats once traveled. The Kissimmee is no exception. Historically, the river meandered approximately 103 miles from beginning to end with a floodplain that was fifty-six miles wide and fell from fifty-six feet at Lake Kissimmee to fifty-one feet at Lake Okeechobee. The river moved very slowly with velocities averaging less than two feet per second. The historic floodplain covered about 35,000 acres of wetland and was home to a wide diversity of fish and wildlife. Ducks and wading birds were everywhere, along with diverse plant life.

Prior to 1940, human habitation was sparse along the river in the Kissimmee basin, but rapid growth and development came after World War II. The public became concerned about flood control, and the state of Florida responded with a request to the federal government to design a flood-control plan for the region.

In 1948, Congress authorized the U.S. Army Corps of Engineers to initiate construction of the Central & Southern Florida Project for flood control. Between 1962 and 1971, the Kissimmee River was canalized and transformed into a series of impounded reservoirs. The once-meandering river was transformed into a fifty-six-mile-long, thirty-foot-deep, and 300-foot-wide canal that is now affectionately called "The Ditch." Much of the valuable floodplain was lost and a lot of the wildlife along the river disappeared (Kissimmee River Restoration History).

Today, a project is under way to return some of the river to its former glory and is touted as the largest river restoration project in history. There is a project being considered for the Apalachicola that would discontinue dredging the river and would seriously hinder barge traffic that is present on the river today. Only time will tell what the outcome will be.

The steamboats are gone and so are some of the rivers they traveled, but what they did for the commerce and progress of Florida should always be remembered, as should the people who made it all happen; they were true pioneers.

2

The Disston Purchase and How Florida Benefited

Hamilton Disston was sometimes thought of as a scoundrel who used to take a drink often with his friends from Philadelphia. He also liked to invest other people's money; although he had plenty of his own that he inherited from his father, Henry S. Disston. Hamilton may have sometimes behaved like a hell-raising, spoiled, rich kid, but he was nonetheless considered a gentleman in most circles. To his credit, he rescued the state of Florida from bankruptcy and made a name for himself that should be remembered by the people of Florida forever. What he did was take a gamble that paid off for him and most of his associates. "Ham," as he was called, was a modern-day entrepreneur the likes of which have been few and far between in the state, even as we know it today. He took a chance and lined his own pockets, but he also gave back by furnishing employment and progress in a place where there was little of either.

Disston's father, Henry, had also made his fortune through his own entrepreneurship in the 1800s in Philadelphia as the founder of the now-famous Disston Saw and Tool Works. He was brought to America by his father who died after they had been in Philadelphia only three days. Henry was fourteen years old at the time and went to work as an apprentice for a saw maker in Philadelphia. The job didn't last long before the saw maker failed, and young Henry was paid off with some unfinished trowels. The industrious young man took the unfinished trowels and finished them. He then sold them to a couple of hardware stores in the area and finally had some money in his pocket and two new customers (Harner, 13–14).

Henry went into business for himself making fine carpenter saws that are still collected today as examples of early craftsmanship. The saws were finished with a heat treatment method that Henry invented to make them stay sharp for a long time. He founded the Keystone Saw, Tool and File Company which later evolved into the Disston Saw and Tool Works that exists today. The company was named in honor of Henry's home state of Pennsylvania, and by 1885 it covered sixty-six acres and employed 8,000 workers. The name Disston was synonymous with quality, reliability, and service to customers in the early days of tool manufacture and still is today (14).

At the time his son Hamilton was born, Henry was twenty-five years old and had rented a shop in Philadelphia. He borrowed $200 to equip it with the first steam-powered saw machinery in the country. Unfortunately, because he was a subtenant in the shop, his landlord seized Henry's equipment for unpaid rent. He was forced to go to work at home making tools until he could buy back his equipment (Iatarola).

Hamilton came into the world on August 23, 1844, and started to work in his father's company while he was still in grade school. By the time he was fifteen years old he had attained the position of full-time apprentice. Company custom established by Henry Disston was that each of his sons was to apprentice for five to seven years before assuming an executive position. This was to ensure that each future leader in the company would have firsthand knowledge of the operational procedures and greater familiarity with his fellow workers. Henry's detailed plans and directions for his business were responsible for it being so successful in later years (Harner, 14).

In 1861, the streets of Philadelphia were filled with marching militia, and fiery speeches were being made everywhere in Pennsylvania because of the start of the Civil War. The war also brought on the factory's rapid expansion because of the immediate need to manufacture materials for the Union Army. A rolling steel mill was constructed and Henry appealed to his workers in the national interest to report defects and suggest possible modifications to enhance their war products. These included knapsack mountings, scabbards, swords, and guns among other things. For those employees who joined the Union Army he gave an additional bonus of 50 percent of their government pay and promised them a secure job after they returned from the war (Iatarola).

Being a patriotic young man and wanting to do something to help his country, Hamilton tried to enlist in the army but was told he was too young. Not giving up, he became a fireman for the Northern Liberties Volunteer Fire Company. They did a lot of drilling and marching and were outfitted with red shirts and blue pants that served as uniforms. Hamilton was satisfied he was doing something to help but ended up going to so many fires it interfered with his work at the company, so his father stepped in and put a stop to his activities (Harner, 14).

After he grew older, Hamilton joined the army twice, but his father paid the enlisting bonuses and brought him back to the factory. He tried to convince his son it was more patriotic to make saws and tools than to be shot at (14).

By now Hamilton was an extremely popular young man among his fellow factory workers, so he and around a hundred others joined the army and declared themselves the "Disston Volunteers." Henry Disston was so proud of his son he reluctantly gave his permission and even equipped the new unit out of his own pocket. Hamilton served as a private in the company. When the volunteers were finally mustered out of the service, their jobs were waiting for them at the factory and the tremendous building boom all over the nation made their saws and tools even more sought after. After the war, Hamilton's apprentice days were over. He was made a junior executive. Still a popular man among his peers, they all called him "Ham," a nickname that stuck with him the rest of his life.

On Ham's twenty-first birthday his father changed the name of the company to Disston & Sons. Henry died in 1878, and Hamilton became president of the company (14). His tenure at the upper echelon of the company began with the firm's most prosperous years. Demands for the many saws they produced intensified as new lines of products were introduced including a whole line of steel files. Hamilton always stayed ahead of his competition when it came to design and technology. The company's success led to a need for more space, so Hamilton looked for a site large enough to build a new factory. The site had already been chosen by Henry Disston before he died. He was familiar with the area's transportation sources and had envisioned an area west of the railroad tracks in Tacony, Pennsylvania, for settlement of his workforce. Henry had purchased 399 acres of land on both sides of the railroad tracks and reserved forty acres for the new factory between the railroad and the Delaware River (Iatarola).

In 1876, the Disston Company started a new community in Tacony with forty-four duplexes and twelve row-style houses they built just west of the railroad tracks. There were even funds set aside for a park, a school, and independent waterworks. In the benefits package for company workers favorable terms were available to buy or rent homes. The deed restrictions of the community encouraged a stable family-oriented atmosphere for everyone. Later, funds were made available and land donated for churches, a music hall, a library, and a scientific society. Hamilton was learning and practicing his community-building ways long before he ever came to Florida (4).

After the company's move to Tacony, Hamilton developed an immediate kinship with his cousin Thomas W. South. South was the local magistrate in 1875 and doubled as the real estate agent for all the properties within the Disston Estate. South virtually oversaw the orderly implementation of the new industrial city at Tacony. It was well known that nothing went on in Tacony without the approval of South and Disston. Although Hamilton had a great interest in politics, he never held public office except for serving for a time as the city's fire commissioner and as the first park commissioner in the 1870s. He did, however, virtually control Republican nominations in the city during the 1870s and 1880s. In addition to controlling Tacony's water source and politics he was the major investor in the Tacony Fuel Gas Company when it formed in 1888. Ten years later the company was wholly owned by Henry Disston and Sons after Jacob Disston bought the company (Iatarola, 6).

When Hamilton's four brothers joined him in the company, he was still president. They were Albert H., Horace C., William, and Jacob Steelman Disston. None of the brothers had the leadership ability or prestige of Hamilton, so he remained the president. It is generally understood that the company's inner workings were left to Hamilton's younger brothers and to his Uncle Samuel during Hamilton's tenure as president. His role was more ceremonial. For example, when President Rutherford B. Hayes visited the plant, Hamilton showed him a rough piece of steel at the beginning of the visit and less than forty-five minutes later presented him with a finished saw with the president's name on it (6).

In the five years after his father's death, Hamilton boosted the company production by 35 percent and became one of the most famous men in the

United States. He also had a passion for fishing and began to make trips to Florida to engage in the sport. It's likely his first view of Florida, in 1877, was over the tip of a fishing rod while trolling the east coast below Jacksonville. The group of men he socialized with were wealthy and owned yachts. They often shared a yacht and headed for Florida or the Florida Keys for their fishing parties. From Hamilton's first trip there he was fascinated with the possibility of reclaiming swampland to facilitate agriculture and possible residential development (Harner, 14).

In the 1800s Florida was thought to need drastic improvement because much of its land area comprised of what was then considered worthless swamp. Not only that, but Florida was for all practical purposes bankrupt. A writer for the *New York Herald* wrote in 1894: "I am confident no sane man who knows what Florida is would give a thousand dollars to gain possession of all the territory beyond the St. Johns River. No decent man would think of living in the state outside of two or three points on the St. Johns and the Gulf." After the War between the States many of the inhabitants of Florida were living in abject poverty mainly in Key West, Tampa, Jacksonville, and Tallahassee. The 1880 census showed 269,000 inhabitants in the state. Railroads were badly needed if progress was to be made, and the state government tried to provide them by giving away state-owned land to a number of people who said they would build the railroads, but they never did. This brought into default a lot of bond issues that were guaranteed by the state. By the time the war was over in 1865, every rail bond ever issued was in default and the state was faced with paying $1 million in interest on some $14 million of bonds. The only other alternative was declaring bankruptcy, which would make the state unable to keep functioning (Harner, 15).

In February 1879, Disston was convinced by one of his friends that the fertile soil and muck land in Florida had great agricultural value, so in 1881 he put together a group of trusted friends and called the company the Atlantic and Gulf Coast Canal and Okeechobee Land Company. They contracted with Florida's Internal Improvement Fund to drain swamplands near Lake Okeechobee. The drainage contract called for reclamation of some 12 million acres of land that would be deeded in plots, beginning after reclamation of the first 200,000 acres, alternately to the state and the land company. He was to repay his friends with half the reclaimed land he had made habitable. Hamilton Disston had a knack for buying things with borrowed money. It sounded like a great deal, but it was also illegal because all the land was tied up in litigation by other bondholders who were demanding $1 million. These bondholders had become alarmed during the years of Republican government when the trustees of the Internal Improvement Fund began disposing of state land at ridiculously low prices that were paid in depreciated scrip. There was also a commitment by the purchasers to bring in settlers and reclaim land, and this was never done. All the purchasers really wanted was the virgin timber, which they proceeded to cut and sell (15).

In 1870, Francis Vose, who was an original investor in bonds of the Florida Railroad, secured a court order forbidding payment for land in anything but U.S. money. When land sales continued without any payments to creditors, Vose and his associates had the lands put in receivership, after which sales could be made only with consent of bondholders like him. Vose bought up other claims and threatened to take over the lands or force a public sale (Harner, 16).

The state's land problem was addressed by Governor William D. Bloxham in 1881. Bloxham, who was lieutenant governor at the time, became the first Democratic governor since the Civil War by carrying thirty-three of thirty-nine counties in the election. The state had been controlled by the Republicans, and the uncertainty of the Republicans' reconstruction policies and the panic of 1873 had brought economic doldrums that would be hard to overcome in the days ahead. Bloxham stressed in his inaugural address the need for immigrants, education, and transportation within the state to achieve growth and prosperity. First he had to deal with the state's fiscal crisis (Tebeau, 278).

In 1881, Hamilton Disston was fishing in Florida with his friend Henry S. Sanford when he was approached by Governor Bloxham in a somewhat secretive agreement to purchase 4 million acres of so-called overflow land at 25 cents per acre. This money would pay the bondholders and clear title to state lands. This would become known as the Disston Purchase, and it was to be the largest purchase of land by a private individual in the nation. His holdings would amount to 6,250 square miles or 4.5 million acres (277). The price of all that land was $1 million, which Disston didn't have and never did pay. In truth, he personally put up only $100,000 to $200,000 of the million. He paid $200,000 to seal the contract, but it was borrowed from friends in Philadelphia. The next payment on the land was not due until December 30, 1882. Much of the property he bought turned out to be high and dry, very desirable land and not the "swamp and overflow land" that was advertised. It is estimated that Disston got at least 150,000 more acres in his land deal with the state than he originally bargained for. This area included future Gulfport and St. Petersburg, Florida (Tebeau, 278).

Governor Bloxham never doubted the wisdom of the sale, but it was to earn him a lot of criticism for a long time. It was said the purchase price was too low, and the rights of squatters and homesteaders were not recognized. Disston had been allowed to select land that wasn't actually swampy or overflowed, and the criticism was that big interests were again being served. In actuality, squatters had two years to pay for the land they were living on at $1.25 per acre, but this was a considerable sum for most Florida squatters (Harner, 16). As the year after the purchase drew to a close, Disston had already opened the waterway from Lake Okeechobee to the gulf via the Caloosahatchee River and a three-mile canal to Lake Hicpochee, and another waterway from Okeechobee to Kissimmee, Florida, via the Kissimmee River. His friends in Philadelphia had originally put up $600,000, but that was rapidly spent with the down payment and the dredging projects going full blast. With only four days left before the Disston Purchase would be declared in default, the resourceful Disston found a way to save the project. He sold two million acres to an Englishman, Sir Edward Reed, for $600,000. Disston now owed the state only $300,000, and his group of investors was again in good financial shape (Tebeau, 278).

Kissimmee City, once called Allendale (now called Kissimmee), was just a small cow town on the north shore of Lake Tohopekaliga, which was the headwaters of the Kissimmee River. Disston decided to build his headquarters there and a house that he and his wife Elizabeth would live in when they were not in Philadelphia. Kissimmee became alive overnight and was hailed by some land speculators as destined to become a great inland seaport. This later came true in 1883 when Disston started a steamboat line that ran from Ft. Myers to Kissimmee. The steamboats were entirely built in Kissimmee by the people there in a huge boatyard that Disston provided. Even the boilers and engines were assembled there. Many of the employees had never seen a ship or a steam engine. A lot of them were local cowboys who had never held a steady job in their lives. Kissimmee was now a very active city because the interior of Florida was opened to the outside world thanks to Disston's efforts (*Osceola County Centennial: 1887–1987*, 3). A railroad also came to Kissimmee in 1882. The city was the southern terminal of the South Florida Railroad. The track was laid through the main street of town known as Broadway. When the track was complete, a station was built in the north part of town. Mrs. Ira Bass arrived in Kissimmee on the first train. Her husband was an employee of Hamilton Disston and came to Kissimmee driving a mule train bringing gear for their new home. Mr. Bass was helping lay out the railroad in the area known as the Sugar Belt line which would eventually become a sugar mill in the new town of St. Cloud just ten miles from Kissimmee. This was another Disston project. Also, in 1883, Henry B. Plant began an extension of the South Florida Railroad and built a connecting narrow-gauge line linking the St. Johns and Kissimmee river valleys to Tampa. This line later became the Atlantic Coast Line Railroad (*Osceola County Centennial: 1887–1987*, 16).

Kissimmee was once called the Tropical City, so when the South Florida Railroad built a hotel in 1883 to accommodate tourists, it was named the Tropical. It was a rambling but elegant hostelry that boasted a six-story observation tower, golf, a boathouse, and boats to be used by its guests. It was a large, handsome building, three and a half stories high, and overlooked the lake. The front of the hotel was 132 feet wide, and it had almost 700 feet of verandahs. The Tropical contained eighty rooms and even had electric bells and every other convenience available in its day for the guests. Many notables enjoyed the hotel's comforts in those days, including President Chester A. Arthur and Mr. and Mrs. John Jacob Astor who were on their honeymoon (64).

Prior to 1884, the city of St. Cloud was a cypress swamp, overflowed much of the time. Efforts were made as early as 1847 to drain the area but this never became a reality until Hamilton Disston came along. After the land was drained, the Sugar Belt Railroad was constructed on the new land that was now seven feet above lake level. Disston's second dredge completed the four-mile-long easterly cut across Cross Prairie to East Lake Tohopekaliga. This lowered the water level in the St. Cloud area around eight feet and made possible the new city. It also made available thousands of acres of new fertile land. The first sugar mill was started by Sam L. Lupfer Sr. from Pennsylvania. He brought in Italian and French workers from Louisiana and had around 350 African Americans working in the fields. Mr. Lupfer later founded the Osceola Hardware Company. At the time, this sugar mill was the largest in the United States and cost $1 million to build and equip.

Hamilton Disston later bought the mill from Lupfer and contracted Captain Rufus E. Rose to build and operate his mill. In 1886 or 1887, Captain Rose asked the guests on his steamboat *Okeechobee* to suggest a name for the new sugar plantation and the name St. Cloud was mentioned. The name stuck, so the city was born.

St. Cloud was only ten miles from Kissimmee, which made it easy to get to and supply from Disston's headquarters. He planted around 20,000 acres of sugarcane there and built another mill on Lake Okeechobee. St. Cloud is now a vital and growing city thanks to the central Florida boom that was started by Disney World. Other cities that were started by Disston's drainage efforts around St. Cloud were Southport, Narcoosee, and Runnymede (*Osceola County Centennial: 1887–1987*, 86–107). Of the three, Runnymede no longer exists. It was east of St. Cloud and was primarily a logging town. Perhaps the only claim to fame it ever had was the three-story Runnymede Hotel that was operated by an eccentric Englishman, Beauchamp Watson. He built his residence, a store, and a few other buildings and tried to start an agricultural school. The hotel catered to northern visitors but was not completed until the Disston Drainage Company took it over and used it as their temporary headquarters. The hotel featured activities such as horseback riding, tennis, croquet, a library, and evening dances. The Sugar Belt Railroad had a depot there. Years after Disston had the hotel, J. Edward Krause of Indianapolis bought the property and added it to his chain of hotels. He did an extensive remodeling of the property and added some guest cottages on the grounds.

The hotel was abandoned in the 1920s. In the 1940s, a cattleman by the name of John J. Padgett bought it and the hotel was dismantled. The lumber from the hotel was used to build fifteen or twenty small houses in Orlando. Runnymede is now classified as a Florida ghost town (Runnymede-Ghost Town).

A new town that never got off the ground was Floridelphia. A brochure circulated in Philadelphia touted the town as being situated in the most healthful, attractive, picturesque, and valuable portion of Florida with unequaled climate, balmy breezes, no frosts or malaria, tropical fruits, flowers, and vegetables. The plan called for the town streets to be laid out much like those in Philadelphia. The streets running north and south would be numbered from First to Twenty-eighth, and from east to west they would be Columbia Avenue to Washington Avenue. Floridelphia was located between Lake Tiger and Lake Kissimmee in Polk County, Florida, and was to be 6,000 acres in size. It was also noted that Floridelphia was on a direct line of communication through the state having water navigation to the Caloosahatchee River, and thence to Charlotte Harbor and the Gulf of Mexico. A steamboat dock was being constructed at the foot of Market Street to be used by a commodious, handsome, fast passenger and freight steamboat. That steamboat, constructed in Kissimmee in 1887, was the *Floridelphia*. She ran for only two tourist seasons before she was sold to a Latin American concern in 1889. The *Floridelphia* finally went to Los Angeles after the Panama Canal was completed. When the city of Floridelphia failed, another dream brought about by the Disston purchase also failed (Bair).

Disston also tried raising rice, but the rich soil caused the rice to grow about five feet tall with such heavy heads of grain the tops fell over before the grain could be harvested. Eventually the rice problem was solved, and he successfully planted around 5,000 acres. Disston donated forty acres of land to the U.S. Department of Agriculture for an experiment on plantings with the rich soil. This became one of the first experiments in scientific agriculture in the United States (Tebeau, 281).

After the trade route from Kissimmee to Ft. Myers was in place, Disston turned his attention to other holdings around the state. The city of Tarpon

4. Passengers aboard the Steamboat *Floridelphia* on Lake Kissimmee. Floridelphia was a settlement on the shore of Lake Kissimmee laid out like Philadelphia, Pennsylvania. Photo used by permission of the Florida Photographic Archives.

Springs was built after he sent a survey crew to lay out the city in 1883. The entire original town was built using lumber from a Disston sawmill in Atlantic City, New Jersey. The lumber was sent to the mouth of the Anclote River by ship and then by barge up the river to Tarpon Springs. Another Tropical Hotel was built in town for all the workers and travelers. It was a smaller version of the one in Kissimmee. Henry Plant had completed a railroad to Tampa, but Tarpon Springs had no good means of transportation between the cities, so Disston established a stagecoach line to bring wealthy northerners to town and establish Tarpon Springs as a winter resort (American Guide Series, 421).

Hamilton then concentrated his efforts on building a city named after him. He set aside 12,000 acres near Boca Ciega Bay that featured wide streets and a large business district. The city was planned for about 50,000 people. Disston City was touted in the northern papers as the place to live with an almost perfect climate. All his friends were invited to the new city on Christmas Eve of 1884 for a huge celebration and to stay in a new hotel he built called the Waldorf.

A steamboat wharf was built in Disston City to accommodate boats that arrived from along the coast and Disston's four steamers. One of these that served Disston City, the *Mary Disston,* was used to deliver mail to Manatee County and passengers and freight to and from Tampa and Cedar Key. This steamboat was named after Disston's mother Mary and was probably the best equipped boat in his fleet. She was designed and built under the supervision of Captain J. W. Toplitt in Pittsburgh, Pennsylvania, around 1884. The boat was 83 feet long. There was a mail contract the boat served in 1889 for the Tampa to Bradenton run, but she missed the mail transfer two out of three times in Tampa and was dismissed. Later the boat was sold to the Orange Belt Railroad and used on the Cedar Key to Tarpon Springs to Clearwater run. One account says the *Mary Disston* caught fire next to the dock in Disston City and was set adrift to sink in the bay. Disston is reported to have had another steamboat named the *Mary Disston,* but not much is known of her.

In 1890, a gentleman by the name of Captain John F. Chase envisaged the possibility of establishing a city where veterans of the Civil War might spend their last days. Since post office officials of the day didn't like the name Disston City, it was changed to Veterans City. A trolley line in 1905 that originated in St. Petersburg also ran to Veterans City. That along with other prosperity caused the town to be incorporated and named Gulfport.

It is known today as the Gateway to the Gulf as it is the point of departure for the Gulf of Mexico. It faces Boca Ciega Bay, which leads to the Gulf (BootsnAll Travel).

By the mid-1800s Hamilton Disston's empire was plagued by problems that left him despondent and worried about financial failure. Many of his Florida investments were not reaping the benefits he envisioned. Some of the land he had drained was not suitable for development of any kind because over-drainage in some areas led to more severe problems in others. The Grover Cleveland administration in 1894 removed a bounty of two cents per pound that was instituted in 1890 to assist domestic sugar production, and there was a nationwide economic panic in 1893. Severe freezes devastated Florida's citrus industry in 1894 and 1895 and caused cash flow problems at his sugar manufacturing company. On top of all that, land prices plummeted. In 1866, Disston offered the owner of the Orange Belt Railroad, Peter Demens, 60,000 acres if the railroad came to Disston City. Demens demanded an additional 50,000 acres and Disston's board of directors balked at the deal. The railroad wound up going to St. Petersburg instead of Disston City. That, along with a yellow fever epidemic that raged within the city, caused many businesses there to move to St. Petersburg. Back in Pennsylvania the Saw Works was forced to reduce wages because of the 1893 economic panic. A note of $1 million that was drawn on the business to finance Disston's Florida operations helped paint a bleak economic picture for Hamilton by 1895. It was becoming increasingly evident that Disston's concept of steamboats and canals was becoming outmoded as the railroads opened up more and more parts of Central Florida. Many of his investors began to realize that they might never see their anticipated returns (Harner, 17).

Although Hamilton Disston was credited with bailing Florida out of bankruptcy and changing it from a wilderness to a prosperous state, few reminders remain today of his far-reaching influence. Gulfport Junior High School changed its name to Disston Junior High School before it finally closed in the 1970s. The area of St. Petersburg known as Disston Heights is centered at 49th street, which was formerly Disston Boulevard. The old Disston Community there boasts a large shopping center and at least a handful of businesses with Disston in the name. The 150,000 acres on the Pinellas County peninsula that once belonged to Disston is the highest ground in the county and is a destination for residents in lower-lying areas when threatened with a hurricane.

Hamilton Disston met an untimely death in 1896 that remains something of a mystery. He went to the theater that night and after returning immersed himself in the bathtub and fired a single shot. There were no eyewitnesses, but a Philadelphia newspaper and a distant nephew of Disston's reported the death as a suicide. Other newspapers across the country reported that he died of a weak heart. The official coroner's report read that he died of natural causes, probably a weak heart.

After Disston's death, his brother William took over the company and borrowed $1 million from James Stokesburg of J. P. Morgan to pay off Hamilton's Florida debts. The brothers had never agreed with Hamilton's Florida vision and were probably glad to be rid of the problem. Cash flow problems persisted at the factory, but recovery and future expansion would occur at the turn of the century. Hamilton Disston's estate was divided among his wife and three sons, Henry, Frank, and Albert. Twenty-seven years after his death, the Hamilton Disston Elementary School in Pennsylvania was opened on land donated by the Disston family (Iatarola).

In Central Florida, Hamilton Disston is recognized as its savior and a true pioneer who opened the way for what is today. If Disston could have seen the impact Disney World has had on the area and the growth of Orlando, he probably would have been proud.

Steamboats on the Kissimmee

The first boats built in Hamilton Disston's shipyard that opened the Kissimmee and the Caloosahatchee rivers to travel were four dredges. Without the dredges the whole drainage project would not have been possible.

Disston *Dredge #1*. This dredge worked during the operation on the lower drainage project out of Lake Okeechobee. The Caloosahatchee River was opened toward the Gulf to Ft. Myers and the St. Lucie canal toward the Atlantic Ocean.

Disston *Dredge #2*. This dredge was used to open up the waterway between Tohopekaliga and East Lake Tohopekaliga. When this canal was finished, the current velocity scooped out the bed of the canal to a depth of several feet below the line of excavation. During the first thirty days, the lake surface fell thirty-six inches and East Lake Tohopekaliga developed a beautiful sand beach. The surrounding marshes changed to rich meadow lands.

Disston *Dredge #3*. This was a suction dredge and opened the deep canal between Lake Tohopekaliga and Lake Cypress called the President's Cut. This deep canal has a swift current today as it flows across Lake Cypress to the headwaters of the Kissimmee River and onto Lake Kissimmee.

Disston *Dredge #4*. This dredge was built in Kissimmee in 1883 and was called a "snag boat." It was equipped with tackle for hoisting logs and other debris from the rivers and canals. The dredge was the first in central Florida to be called a snag boat and was used everywhere drainage was happening (Hetherington, 25–26).

By 1884, Disston's Florida Land Improvement Company and the Kissimmee Land Company were moving ahead at amazing speed for the time and the reclamation effort progressed steadily. The report of State Engineer H. S. Duval stated that over 2 million acres had been permanently drained in the area.

To navigate the serpentine Kissimmee River the steamboats had to be of a very special design. Most were about 40 feet long with a beam of 10 to 14 feet, and the paddle wheel used for propulsion produced a shower of water that brought the name "wet tail steamboats" into existence. Later boats had doors that enclosed the wheel and kept the stern relatively dry. As navigation became better, the boats tended to be larger so they could haul more cargo.

The construction of numerous steamboats in Kissimmee began in 1881 and was a bustling industry. The boats were needed to supply the dredges and remote settlements. Company officials also needed transportation to reach their work areas. The boats used lumber—mostly pine and cypress from the local area—in their construction.

Most of the boats that plied the Kissimmee Waterway were built in Kissimmee at Disston's Okeechobee Shipyard or by individuals living near there. The shipyard had a foundry and a machine shop. These were used to fabricate metal parts used in the boats. Most of the boilers and engines came from Orlando, although a few were made in Kissimmee. Among the original workers at the yard were "Bunk" Tyson, the head carpenter, and Captain Clay Johnson, the supervisor. A Captain Cochran was the Disston engineer in 1882 (Cantrell, 8).

Early Kissimmee is remembered as having three sawmills. They were near the foot of what is today Drury Street. In those days the street was called Ingram. One of the mills belonged to Major J. H. Allen and another probably belonged to Archibald Bass, a relative of mine. That mill was near where the present-day boat basin is located. The third sawmill was between Penfield and Mound streets. These sawmills were working as hard as they could making lumber for the boatyards and for people who were camping all over town waiting for lumber to build houses and businesses (8).

There were also several docks in the area. One belonged to Major J. H. Allen and was near his sawmill. Another longer dock ran out in front of the old Tropical Hotel. The third dock was south of the Tropical and was marked "Bass" and owned by the Bass family. The Okeechobee Shipyard dock was next. Beside that was a dock that belonged to Captain Clay Johnson and his family. The first city dock was at the foot of Ruby Avenue and was destroyed by a hurricane. The new city dock had wide ramps and a large covered pavilion where dances were held. This was also swept away by a hurricane, but the foundation was still used by steamboats. It eventually became the foundation for the Kissimmee Yacht Club (*Osceola County Centennial: 1887–1987*, 395–396).

There is a Kissimmee Historical Trail that can be visited today, and some of the old houses and business sites of early Kissimmee are still there. The Osceola County Historical Society located on Bass Road in Kissimmee has a museum and research center with a wealth of information about the early town and the steamboats.

Many of the boats we know of were built in Kissimmee or came there from other places but were used exclusively on the river or in Lake Tohopekaliga.

Mamie Lown was built in 1888 somewhere in the Midwest. She was a small side-wheeler that was about 28 feet long with a beam of 8 feet. Her primary use was to haul machinery for the sugar mill on East Lake Tohopekaliga. *Mamie Lown* had a sister ship called the *Shipman* that was about the same size.

The *Cincinnati* was built in Chicago in 1889 and originally was 34.6 feet long with a beam of 9.9 feet and drew 3.4 feet of water under way. This boat was rebuilt and called *Roseada* in 1893 by Captain Clay Johnson. It was named after his two daughters, Rose and Ada. The rebuilt boat was 57 feet long with a beam of 14.7 feet and drew 3.3 feet of water. This boat lasted until the 1920s and was used mostly for the Kissimmee to Ft. Basinger run. From 1917 to 1920 she was used around Lake Okeechobee. From 1920 until around 1928 she was used by the Kissimmee Island Cattle Company, "KICCO," to haul supplies. *Roseada* was finally abandoned after a hurricane drove her ashore in Kissimmee in 1928.

The *Lillie* was built in 1900 for passenger service to Ft. Myers. There are no dimensions for *Lillie*, but she was a double-deck boat and often carried sightseers around Tohopekaliga when not being used for passenger service. The cabins had double deck bunks with blue checked sheets and pillow cases. There were also blue blankets on the beds. The doors to the cabins had china door knobs as did all the other doors. On the pilot house

5. There was a water tower that could be seen just after you round a curve in the river at Kicco. There was also an old schoolhouse; both are now gone—the last remains of steamboat days on the Kissimmee River. Photo from the Bass Photo Collection.

above the bell was a set of deer horns that was supposed to signify that she was the fastest boat around. This was another boat that belonged to Captain Clay Johnson. All his boats had deer horns above the bell. The *Lillie* ran until 1926 and was finally converted to a houseboat.

The *Osceola* was built in Kissimmee in 1910 and was 74.6 feet long with a beam of 21.1 feet. She drew 3.6 feet of water. This boat could haul 1,000 boxes of oranges and still make 12 miles per hour while under way. She was primarily a freight boat.

The *Rosedele* was built in Kissimmee in 1910 and was 50 feet long with

6. The *Lillie* and the *Osceola* floating together in Lake Kissimmee. Both were called "wet tail steamboats" because the paddle wheel threw water on the stern. Photo used by permission of the Florida Photographic Archives.

a beam of 15 feet. She only drew 1.6 feet of water while under way and was considered a shallow water boat. The *Rosedele* was propeller driven and used primarily for showing tourists land that was for sale at Alligator Bluff and Micco Bluff that was owned by the Hunter Land Company.

Lucy B. was probably the last boat built in Kissimmee and was 50 feet long with a 12-foot beam. She drew 3 feet of water. Built for freight and passenger service, she was converted to a houseboat sometime in the mid-1920s.

Mary Belle was probably built in Kissimmee by Major J. H. Allen in one of his sawmills. She was operating on the lakes prior to 1882 and could have been one of the first. A small steamer, she was 47 feet long with a beam of 10 feet. The boat drew 3.5 feet of water while under way. *Mary Belle* later became *Gertrude* and was owned by Captain Tom Bass. *Gertrude* was named after one of Bass's daughters.

Spray was built in Kissimmee sometime in 1882. She was 40 feet long with a 10-foot beam. The boat had a narrow hull and was a side-wheeler. *Spray* had a bad habit of listing to one side or the other and also had a bad boiler. She was the steamboat most closely connected with settlers in the St. Cloud and Narcoosee area. The boat was owned by Archibald Bass and W. J. Brack, who also operated it. She was beached in 1893 in Kissimmee and finally burned.

Colonist was built in Kissimmee in 1885. The boat was 45 feet long with a beam of 13.7 feet. She drew 5.5 feet of water, which sometimes made it difficult for her to operate in shallow parts of the lake. The boat was named for the English settlement at Narcoosee and operated between Kissimmee and Narcoosee until the Sugar Belt Railroad served those two points. After the railroad came, the boat was sold to Captain Ben Hall who wore it out in service on the Kissimmee River.

Narcoosee was built either in Kissimmee or Narcoosee in 1884 or 1885. Captain Hall first applied for vessel documentation in 1885, listing the boat as 106 tons. There are no dimensions available on this boat.

Sadie was built in Salem, Massachusetts, and was sometimes known as *Sadie of Salem*. Built in 1886 she was 61.7 feet long with a beam of 14.8 feet. *Sadie* drew 4.9 feet of water while under way. She was a propeller tug and couldn't get around tight corners like a stern-wheeler could.

Floridelphia was a large two-decked stern-wheeler built in Kissimmee in 1887 but sold to a Latin American concern in May 1889. The boat was a rather large 85 feet long and proved to be too large for the shallow waters she encountered. This boat was built under the auspices of the Floridelphia Steamship Company and finished in 1887. The *Floridelphia* ran most of the time to Kramer Island in Lake Kissimmee, where the company attempted to build a tourist town patterned after Philadelphia, Pennsylvania. The venture failed, so the boat eventually wound up in California after the Panama Canal was built.

Tallulah was later named *Reindeer*. She was 33 feet long and no other dimensions are known. Built in Kissimmee in 1881, the boat ran locally until 1901 when she was abandoned.

The *J. M. Kreamer* was named after Disston's civil engineer. She was 33 feet long, had a beam of 15 feet, and a draft of 2.4 feet. The boat was built in 1894. Jim Gilbert was her captain for a short period of time in 1895 and 1896. The *Kreamer* was a small private boat, not used on any particular route.

Hamilton Disston #1 was the first Disston boat. She never got to Kissimmee because she drew too much water to make it that far. However, some steamboat history placed her in Kissimmee at one time.

Hamilton Disston #2 was much smaller than *#1*. The boat was 48.6 feet long and had a beam of 14.2 feet. This boat drew 3.2 feet of water. Built in 1889, it had a steel hull that was cut out in Philadelphia and later assembled in Kissimmee. Her upper works were also finished in Kissimmee. Most of her life was spent at the dock because of her poor design. She was built as a party and pleasure boat but was rather a complete flop. She had a wide deck housing compared to her rather narrow hull (four-foot overhang) and had an open forward deck. Even in moderate swells she would take on water over the bow. She had a rather limited freeboard and this, in addition to making her relatively unseaworthy, allowed for little cargo capacity. Thomas A. Edison once selected her for a journey to Ft. Myers where he had a winter home, but the *Hamilton Disston* got stuck in the Southport Canal. Edison, despairing of getting to Ft. Myers, went aboard the *Tallulah* going in the opposite direction back to Kissimmee and continued his journey by railroad.

Octavia was built in Kissimmee in 1891. She was 55 feet long and a freighter. The boat was owned by the Brown Brothers until transferred to service on the Suwannee River. She was later moved to Tampa in 1883 and went into service there.

The *City of Athens* was built in Kissimmee in 1890 and 1891 by the Gilbert brothers and was 65 feet long with a beam of 16 feet. She drew 3.7 feet of water and was a double-deck stern wheeler. There were six staterooms on the upper deck. The boat later burned at Fort Thompson on the Caloosahatchee from a fire caused by hot ashes in her boiler. She was later refloated and rebuilt by the Menge brothers.

Success was built in Kissimmee in 1906. Fifty-six feet long with a beam of 14.5 feet, this boat drew only 2.7 feet of water, making her a shallow water boat. The boat was built by Captain Tom Bass Jr. and Aaron Bronson for the catfish business on Lake Okeechobee. She later took fish to Ft. Myers from Okeechobee.

Basinger was built in Kissimmee in 1899 and was 66.7 feet long with a beam of 17.3 feet. She drew 2.8 feet of water. Used for the Ft. Basinger to Kissimmee run, she could make it in two days because of her speed, almost 12 miles per hour.

Naoma #1 was built in Kissimmee in 1892. She was 40 feet long with a 10-foot beam. She had bevel gears and was a side-wheeler. The shaft was below and chains were run on deck through wheels and a chain drive and connected to a pinion that connected to the side wheels. She was very successful and ran for around five years.

Naoma #2 was built in 1897 in Tampa as both a side-wheeler and a stern-wheeler. She used the engines of *Naoma #1*. Later her engines were removed and put in a boat named *Irene* and she was rebuilt and named the *City of Basinger* to run on the Kissimmee. Captain Carl Buckles ran her and carried freight, but she was generally an unsatisfactory boat and lasted only a short time. Her engines were again removed and put in a boat called *Ruthie*. Nothing is known of *Ruthie*, but *Irene* was a sharpie sailboat until she became the steamboat *City of Basinger*. A sharpie sailboat is described as sharpened at both bow and stern.

Naoma #3 was built in 1900 in Kissimmee and was 55.4 feet long with a beam of 12.2 feet. She drew 2.4 feet of water.

Corona was built in Alva, Florida, by Captain Ben Hall Jr. and his son Edward in 1908. The boat was 57 feet long with a beam of 10.6 feet. She drew 3 feet of water and was built on a river bank in Alva very close to the water. After her topsides were done the rays of the sun literally baked one side of her and the topside planks shrank, causing large cracks to develop. Hall filled up the cracks by driving cedar shingles into them, wedging them in place, and then sawing them off flush. *Corona* kept the shingles all her life. Hall even employed a salt box inside the hull to try and keep the moisture content uniform and halt further expansion and contraction. He kept the boat until after World War I when he sold his interest to the Menge brothers. The boat was originally built for a mail run on the Caloosahatchee to LaBelle. The boat was active until around 1915.

Juanita was built in 1905 in Kissimmee by the Mobley brothers. She was a stern-wheeler with a length of 46 feet and a beam of 15 feet. Her draft was 2.4 feet. The boat was primarily a freight vessel. She was wrecked in December of 1912 and sank because she was overloaded. The cargo shifted to one side and the boat took on water and flipped over. The sinking put a heavy financial burden on the Mobleys. Even though she was raised and refitted, the brothers lost her in the process (*Osceola County Centennial: 1887–1987*, 390–402).

Probably the most legendary figure in Kissimmee's long list of steamboat captains was Clay Johnson. He came from Gretna, Louisiana, near New Orleans in 1883. He was invited to Kissimmee by his brother-in-law, Captain Rufus E. Rose, who was Hamilton Disston's general superintendent. Captain Johnson's first job was superintendent of Disston's shipyard. He was also responsible for the experimental farm at Southport. Some of the sugarcane from the farm was taken to the Cotton Centennial in New Orleans in 1885. The cane won first prize in yield and quantity.

Clay Johnson ran the Kissimmee River from the 1880s to the 1920s, and his steamboating days continued long after most of the river traffic had given way to the railroads and the automobile. In 1917, Captain Johnson moved his operations to the Lake Okeechobee area to haul vegetables, building material, and machinery. Johnson even hauled by steamboat and barge the material that was used to build Conner's Highway from Okeechobee to West Palm Beach during the boom days.

Captain Johnson's first steamboat was the *Mamie Lown*. He also owned the *Black Witch,* a sailboat used as a trading vessel. Johnson built and owned the *Rosalie* in Kissimmee in 1884. She was a steam launch capable of carrying freight and had accommodations for ten passengers. *Rosalie* was 41.1 feet long with a beam of 12.91 feet and a draft of 3.5 feet. She had a stern-wheel and a Westinghouse engine with an upright boiler and could travel around seven miles an hour. The official number of the *Rosalie* was 110662, and her gross tons were 22.66. Some say the *Rosalie* was built by the Disston shipyard, but I believe Captain Johnson built her.

7. Captain Clay Johnson of Kissimmee is pictured on the far left standing with a group of passengers on one of his boats. Johnson closely resembled Mark Twain and was one of the most famous captains on the Kissimmee. Photo used by permission of the Florida Photographic Archives.

If you can picture a tall straight man with a big white moustache across his tanned face, keen blue eyes, and a head of snowy hair covered by a battered boatman's hat, you would have a pretty accurate picture of Clay Johnson. Some folks said he looked just like Mark Twain. He took steamboats where there weren't any buoys or beacons and had no searchlight to point the way at night. There was no ship-to-shore radio in those days to use in case of trouble. A steamboat captain had to be a very resourceful person just to keep the boat moving and all the equipment operating. He also had to be able to read the water ahead like a book. He had to know the difference between a wind ripple and a sandbar or a hidden snag. A good captain knew the river changed shape in fog or mist, and he had to know the way at night. Perhaps all this knowledge helped to shape Clay Johnson into the man he was. He always liked to talk and would delay leaving a steamboat stop if he got in a good conversation. Sometimes he was asked to play the fiddle, and he was the instigator of many a dance, or frolic as they were called back then.

Clay was not without his faults and was especially noted for his profanity, as were most of the old steamboat captains. It seems that profanity was just part of the business. A story from the Osceola County Centennial yearbook tells of one occasion when a squall came up as Clay was towing a barge across a lake. The barge broke loose from the steamboat and drifted toward a lee shore. Clay shook his fist at the heavens and let loose an especially juicy lot of choice epithets and then threw a handful of change into the teeth of the gale to pay off the water gods and change his luck. Such blasphemy must have tempted the Almighty, but no bolt of lightning was dispatched to settle the issue. In spite of his faults, Clay Johnson was a warm-hearted and generous man. If he had collected all the debts owed him, he probably could have retired a wealthy man (*Osceola County Centennial: 1887–1987*, 390–392).

Benjamin Franklin Hall Jr. had the honor of bringing in the largest boat ever to travel up the Kissimmee waterway. The boat was the *Bertha Lee.* After a hazardous trip that took fifty-two days—from New Orleans and up the Caloosahatchee and Kissimmee rivers—he finally took the boat to the Apalachicola River and ran cotton on her until she was wrecked. Hall had just spent $10,000 to refurbish the boat and the wreck left him without any money. He returned to Kissimmee and was later involved in the steamboat business with his son Edward (394–398).

The Halls' greatest success was with three unique vessels all named

Naoma. The older Hall called the craft Naomi, the biblical name, but people confused the "I" with the number "1," so he altered the name to Naoma. These boats ran for around fifteen years starting with the first one that was built in 1892. This boat was unusual in that she had beveled gears and the shaft was down below. Chains were run to the shaft on deck via wheels and chain drive that connected to a pinion gear to turn the side wheels. *Naoma #1* was around for five or six years and was run by Captain Hall. Number two was a rather versatile craft that could be run both as a side-wheeler and a stern-wheeler. *Naoma #2* used the engines from #1 and was probably built in Tampa in 1897. The Halls had a remarkable facility for adaptation and resourceful use of steamboat machinery to both build and keep their vessels running. *The Naoma #2*'s job was to pull or push barges of building materials for a power generating plant that was being built in Sulphur Springs. A very low clearance was needed to pass under a bridge across the river between the power plant and the source of the building supplies. The resourceful Halls built a hinged pilot house on *Naoma #2* that could be lowered along with the smokestacks to pass safely under the bridge. Even so, they had to wait for low tide before going under the steel trolley bridge. After the power generating station was completed, the *Naoma #2* came back to Kissimmee. She was changed into a stern-wheeler and put on the run to Ft. Basinger. The side-wheel equipment was not wasted. It was installed in a sailboat of the sharpie type and named *Irene*. *Irene* was converted to a steamboat and became the *City of Basinger*. Naoma #2 proved to be too fast as a stern-wheeler and too small for the run. She had to tow a barge to carry enough cargo. Finally, after four or five years, Naoma #2 was given up.

The newest and fastest boat on the river in 1900 was Clay Johnson's *Lillie*. To keep up with the competition, Ben Hall built *Naoma #3* in 1901. She was a stern-wheeler and somewhat like the *Lillie* except that the wheelhouse on the boiler deck was raised three feet higher than the cabin roof that extended all the way aft. This raised pilot house enabled the pilot to see the water immediately behind the boat when backing up. This was a big advantage since a lot of time was spent backing up or down the channel to remove water hyacinths on the Kissimmee or to fan the channel during low water periods. Ben Hall ran the *Naoma #3* as captain, and his son Edward worked as engineer on board until the end of 1907. The *Naoma #3* carried some notable passengers in her time.

Napoleon Bonaparte Broward was a steamboat captain on the St. Johns

River during his younger days. Broward later became governor of Florida and based some of his campaign on the issue of draining the Everglades, a project that had been neglected since the cessation of Disston activities in the area. Before the election, he took an inspection trip on the *Naoma #3* to Lake Okeechobee. After the election, he returned as governor and brought many state officials with him. This trip was also on *Naoma #3*. When they reached Taylor Creek, the stream connecting Okeechobee City and the lake, they were running out of fuel for the boat. Since none was available, the governor took off his coat and along with the crew began to cut wood for fuel. Thomas Edison and his family also boarded *Naoma #3* for a ten-day fishing trip around Lake Okeechobee and up Fisheating Creek (*Osceola County Centennial: 1887–1987*, 401–402).

Captain Edward H. Hall was born in Kissimmee in 1884 and was the son of Benjamin Franklin Hall Jr. He grew up on steamboats. They figured so prominently in his life that he took and passed examinations for pilot and engineer in steamboats powered by steam, gasoline, and diesel when he was twenty-one years old. Because he was qualified for any position on the boats, he was able to find employment on the Kissimmee River boats until World War I when he went to sea with the War Shipping Board. He later skippered boats in the Jacksonville area on the St. Johns River.

In World War II Captain Hall served as a commander in the merchant marine and on army transports to Japan. He served in the Normandy invasion and in the Korean War. He was another pioneer with all the skills and knowledge it took to operate the old steamboats (394).

Rufus Edward Rose was a thirty-four-year-old steamboat captain and chemist when he came to Kissimmee from New Orleans. He was to become Hamilton Disston's right-hand man in his operations there. Rose became superintendent of the Disston Everglade Drainage Company and the Disston-St. Cloud Sugar Company. He was also an advisor in the shipbuilding business since he had boats on the Mississippi and Red rivers. Rose had also helped establish the first artificial ice plant in New Orleans and had been instrumental in designing and erecting sugar mills in Louisiana. Rufus Rose was once the owner of the Kissimmee steamboat *Rosalie* and was connected with others that had run the river (*Osceola County Centennial: 1887–1987*, 396).

Thomas Alexander Bass was a relative of mine who figured prominently in the development of Kissimmee and was also a great steamboat skipper. Tom was the son of Joe Everett Bass who was my grandfather. Born July

17, 1855, in Tattnall County, Georgia, he was the fifth of seven children. His father was sheriff of Irwin County, Georgia, for eight years and sheriff of Clinch County, Georgia, for three years after the Civil War. The family moved to Kissimmee in 1872. Tom married his third cousin Missouri Bass in 1872. The 1885 census of Florida listed his occupation as ship carpenter and his wife Missouri as owner of a steamboat. Some stories say Tom Bass took the first steamboat down the Kissimmee to Lake Okeechobee, but I think that story has been confused with another that is related about the first trip to the settlements of Narcoosee and Runnymede. The canal there opened the way from Lake Tohopekaliga to East Lake Tohopekaliga. Captain Rose of the Okeechobee Drainage Project wanted the honor of making the first trip through the new canal and had put a log dam across it. Captain Paul Gibson and Bass went to the dam in a buggy and tried to pull it apart, but it was too big a job for them. Rose came along later, opened the canal, and took his steamboat through. I have not been able to find information as to who made the first actual trip down the Kissimmee after the waterway was opened.

Tom Bass owned several steamboats during his time in Kissimmee, one of which was the *Narcoosee* that was named after the town. He was also made the first sheriff and mayor of Kissimmee. Tom died April 17, 1917, and is buried in Avon Park, Florida (*Osceola County Centennial: 1887–1987*, 34–35).

All the men mentioned as great steamboat captains had a lot in common as individuals. They had the vision and the grit to compete with each other and to help build the steamboat industry in central Florida from nothing to a great enterprise that helped develop the state. They were the men who took the chances and sometimes failed in their endeavors, but the industry flourished because of them, and their names became a part of history. There were others not mentioned here who were also important in claiming the land and rivers of central Florida. Their stories are written down somewhere and should be brought to the forefront of history so they can also be remembered.

The route down the Kissimmee was long and hazardous. After the boats left Kissimmee, it took about five days to run the river to Ft. Basinger and back. By road the trip was a distance of eighty miles, but by steamboat it was 162 miles and sometimes nearly 175. The first stop on the route was Southport, a distance of twelve miles. It was on the south shore of Lake Tohopekaliga and is today the location of a lock that is used for flood control.

Shell Hammock came next, a distance of twenty-five miles. Next was Ft. Gardiner at twenty-seven miles. This old fort was built during the Seminole Indian Wars and is located on the river near present day Camp Mack. The town of Rosalie was on the opposite side of the river from the fort, and the steamboats would load and unload at the dock attached to the commissary there. The commissary supplied groceries and other goods to the local people and contained a post office as well. Mail was delivered by passengers on the steamboats until the actual post office was established. The post office began operation on July 4, 1906, and continued its duties there until March 30, 1918. The mail was then brought to Rosalie by horseback from Bartow. A Mr. Gandy would leave Rosalie and ride all day to Bartow, spend the night, and then return the next day. He made three trips a week. Rosalie is not often mentioned as a steamboat stop, but it was.

The next stop was Shivers at thirty-five miles, followed by Jack Hancock at forty miles. I believe these places were named for pioneers who lived on the shore of Lake Kissimmee, but I don't have any information to prove it.

Across Lake Kissimmee we came to Grape Hammock, a distance of forty-five miles. There was a steamboat landing on one side of the river and the Headwater Inn on the other side. Grape Hammock was where I purchased my house boat in 1986. Curtis Chandley and his wife Barbara own the fish camp there and their family has been present on the river for many years. The old Headwater Inn building where passengers waited for the boats is still standing on the other side of the river.

We entered the river again here and traveled to Rattlesnake Hammock, a distance of sixty miles. The pioneer family of Elijah Godwin lived here for many years, and their home was a steamboat stop. His house and some of the outbuildings were still there when I started traveling the Kissimmee back in 1986. They have since been leveled by the South Florida Water Management District because they were afraid someone would get hurt in the old structures. The Florida Trail runs right through the property. A sign there says, "Rattlesnake Hammock, treat the water," and some old cattle dipping vats are still there from the tick fever days in Florida.

Next, we came to Orange Hammock and a little later to Leander Underhill. Another early Florida pioneer lived here. The mileage is now seventy-six miles from Kissimmee.

At mile eighty-five we found Fort Kissimmee in the Avon Park Bombing Range. It was another Seminole Indian War fort that was established in 1852. The remains of the military cemetery at Fort Kissimmee are still visible. It is a long way from anywhere and the only way to see it is to hike the Kissimmee River section of the Florida Trail. You can get on the trail at River Ranch Resort near Lake Wales, but it is a thirty mile hike to Fort Kissimmee. The only other way to get there is by boat on the river or through the Avon Park Bombing Range. You may have to obtain permission from the Avon Park Bombing Range to visit the fort site and cemetery because of military operations that may be going on there. This is one of the few active military installations that include the site of a Second Seminole War fort. There was also a ferry crossing that went across the river to another Bass family that lived in the area. Long Hammock was at mile ninety.

In 1870 Henry L. Parker was a native of Columbia County, Florida, who later settled at Bluff Hammock where he operated a ferry. After a short time, he moved to Ft. Basinger and settled on the east side of the river. I don't know who operated the steamboat stop after Parker moved to Basinger. Parker was appointed county judge of Brevard County in 1874.

The steamboat stop at Bluff Hammock was at mile 110. The next stop was at Micco Bluff at mile 125.

8. My houseboat *Linda Gale*, anchored near Ft. Kissimmee. Photo from the Bass Photo Collection.

Pearce's stop was at 145 miles. Captain John Mizell Pearce settled on the western side of the Kissimmee River and was a cattleman from Polk County. He had a ferry operation there for many years.

The next stop was Lanier's, another pioneer. It was 150 miles to Lanier's.

We finally arrived at Ft. Basinger at 160 miles and west Basinger at 162 miles. From Ft. Basinger it was only a short distance on to Lake Okeechobee and on to the Caloosahatchee River and finally Ft. Myers (Hetherington, 49).

In 1899 the *Kissimmee Valley Gazette* newspaper described the trip from Kissimmee to Basinger:

> There is no more pleasant way of spending a week than to take the trip to Basinger. Birds of all kinds are in sight the whole way; flocks of ducks, coots, herons, cranes, limpkins, curlews, plume birds and water turkeys without end. There were also alligators, rabbits and water snakes and plenty of fish too. In its narrowness, in the rampant growth of water plants along its low banks, in the unbroken flatness of the landscape, in the labyrinth of by-channels and cut-offs and above all in the appalling, incredible, bewildering crookedness of its serpentine body, it is indeed an extraordinary river.

Ft. Basinger was the final stop for three steamers from Kissimmee when river traffic was at its height. Major J. H. Allen built the steamer *Mary Belle* and was probably the first to make regular weekly trips to Basinger. The *Basinger* and later the *City of Basinger* were two other boats that made the round trip to Kissimmee. The *Basinger* was built in 1892 and could make a speed of twelve miles an hour. She had six staterooms and a crew of six: the captain, engineer, fireman, cook, and two deckhands. The boat hauled freight such as alligator hides, otter and raccoon skins, oranges and grapefruit, and supplies for the ranchers and pioneers all along the river route (*Osceola County Centennial: 1887–1987*, 401).

The dependence on steamboats along the Kissimmee lasted until around 1926, when roads were developed in the area.

In 1915, Basinger's population began to decline when the Kissimmee Valley extension of the Florida East Coast Railroad came to a point twelve miles north of the town. Many of the residents moved to Okeechobee and other nearby communities.

The story of steamboats on the Kissimmee River wouldn't be complete without relating the tale of the *Bertha Lee*. By the mid-1880s, as the dredging activities increased, a reasonably good passage to Lake Okeechobee and the Caloosahatchee had been established and the smaller steamers could go from there to Ft. Myers. Service had begun from Kissimmee to Ft. Basinger and then to Ft. Myers, so Ed Douglas of Kissimmee, acting for the Okeechobee and Gulf Stream Navigation Company, was shopping for a steamboat in the Ohio Valley. There he found the *Bertha Lee*. There was an influx of tourists to Kissimmee and the boat seemed just the one to handle them when viewed alongside others on the Ohio River.

Bertha Lee started life as a western river boat in Portsmouth, Ohio. She was registered as a two-decked stern-wheeled steamboat of 121 gross tons. She was 130 feet long with a beam of 21 feet and drew 3.8 feet of water while under way. The official number of *Bertha Lee* was 3096. The boat was owned by a consortium of Kentuckians for most of her career and was employed by the Louisville and Evansville Mail Company for a mail run between these two cities. Although the *Bertha Lee* was not a small boat by Kissimmee River standards, she was such a bargain that Douglas bought her anyway.

Now he was faced with the task of getting the boat back to Kissimmee via the Ohio and Mississippi Rivers. When the boat got to New Orleans, Douglas hired Benjamin Franklin Hall Jr. as master for the remainder of the trip. Hall had prior experience on the New Orleans to Port Eads run on the Mississippi but had always wanted to visit Florida. He knew little about the hazardous run from New Orleans and around the Gulf of Mexico, and no one on board was familiar with the navigational problems they would encounter once they entered the Caloosahatchee and Kissimmee.

The boat took on a cargo of grain in New Orleans and left there on September 20, 1883, to cross the Gulf. After they entered the Caloosahatchee, the going got tough. It was rather difficult to get a 130-foot boat that drew 3.8 feet of water up the narrow and crooked river. Past Ft. Thompson they encountered shallow and muddy Lake Flint and Bonnet Lake and finally reached Reedy Canal. Just as the boat neared Lake Okeechobee, she really got hung up in Three Mile Canal. A small earthen dam was constructed and the extra water provided when the dam was released allowed the boat to enter Lake Okeechobee. They tied up at Observation Island and cut wood because only three cords were left and more would be needed to cross the lake.

An easy trip was made across the lake, but when they entered the Kissimmee, all that changed. The river was a snake's dream of heaven. It was a crooked combination of curves in confounding numbers. At the time, anything larger than a row boat would have had tough going on the Kissimmee. Many times the *Bertha Lee* had to cut her own channel across some of the sharper bends by using her paddle wheel to generate enough current to cause a scouring action to cut the channel. She would have to turn around, reverse direction, and use the wheel to clear the way. There were also overhanging tree limbs that had to be removed and snags in the river. All this was done by hand and hard labor. After fifteen heartbreaking days the boat finally reached Lake Kissimmee and was very close to being out of food. They dispatched a row boat to go to Kissimmee and meanwhile subsisted on some wild turkeys they bought from passing Indians until the rowboat returned a week later.

It took fifty-two days for the *Bertha Lee* to reach Kissimmee after she entered the Caloosahatchee River. It was probably the longest voyage up the river in history.

Bertha Lee was not the outstanding success that it was hoped to be. The boat was used briefly for moonlight excursions around Lake Tohopekaliga and trips to islands in the lake. Two of her crew, Ben Hall and John Gottwallis, married two sisters they had met on one of the moonlight cruises in a double wedding, so the cruises were not a total loss. Captain Hall finally took the *Bertha Lee* to the Suwannee River, where she ran from Cedar Key to Branford hauling passengers and freight. After awhile, the boat was moved to the Apalachicola and Chattahoochee Rivers, where she made successful cotton runs from Columbus, Georgia, to Apalachicola, the site of her eventual wreck. (*Osceola County Centennial: 1887–1987*, 396–397).

Captain Hall figured in another enterprise in August of 1904. After the trip with the *Bertha Lee* to Kissimmee, he financed a couple of trotline camps at the mouth of the river on Lake Okeechobee. The following winter Hall set up three more camps. This was the start of catfishing activity on Lake Okeechobee that would eventually become a thriving industry for the area. It was no feat to catch as many as eight to ten tons of catfish in a single haul of the nets in those days. Captain Hall picked up the fish from these camps in his steamer *Naoma #2,* which pushed a barge on which was built a refrigerated fish box. At first these fish had to make the long trip on the crooked Kissimmee River all the way to Kissimmee, and Hall was lucky if some didn't spoil along the way. Later, an ice plant was built in Ft. Myers, and he made twice weekly trips to that town instead. It was said that he paid 5 cents a pound for the fish from the camps and doubled his money when they reached their destination. The same year Hall started his fish camps, the O.K. Fish Company was begun on Lake Okeechobee by Fernando Miller. This man was born in Gardner, Illinois, but in 1900 had settled in LaBelle on the Caloosahatchee River. The railroad had reached Ft. Myers in 1904, and a man by the name of C. R. Ward had moved his fishhouse from Punta Gorda and built an ice plant there. Ward was the backer of Miller's O.K. Fish Company on Lake Okeechobee.

The O.K. Fish Company employed about twenty-five men and owned eighteen boats, but in 1909 the price of catfish fell below 3 cents a pound and the O.K. Fish Company ceased operations (Will, 114–116).

Another unsuccessful operator was Dexter Summerlin from Bartow. In 1905, he was hauling fish up the river from the lake to Kissimmee with a launch called *Four Hundred* and a barge. For some reason he also ceased his operation.

Even though Benjamin Hall started the catfish business and was the first, another man turned out to be the biggest operator of them all. That man was Thomas A. Bass from Kissimmee. I do not think this was the same Thomas Bass mentioned in earlier parts of this chapter, but it could have been one of his sons.

Tom Bass first tried his luck fishing in Lake Kissimmee as early as 1905 and later had a crew working on Lake Hicpochee. From here, the fish were carried all the way to Kissimmee. His steamboat had two crews and ran day and night stopping only to take on fuel. It was too long a haul from Lake Hicpochee to Kissimmee because if something went wrong, like grounding, the fish would surely all be spoiled. Tom Bass began his big operation in 1906 when J. S. Bronson, a wealthy cattleman, backed him in the Okeechobee Fish and Fur Company. The *Ft. Myers News Press* on December 8, 1905 announced "Captain T. A. Bass of Kissimmee was here to arrange to ship fish the rest of the year. He has invested $9,000.00 in boats and nets and expects to employ 150 men. He has purchased the steamer *Four Hundred* and has launched a new boat in Kissimmee." This new boat was the 56-foot steamer *Success,* which held two fish boxes, one for catfish and the other for scale fish.

The *Success* brought her first load of fish to Ft. Myers on February 8, 1906. That first load was 6,000 pounds. With the O.K. Fish Company still operating at that time, this was the beginning of a million dollar, fabulous, and colorful era of the catfishing days of Lake Okeechobee.

Captain Bass kept setting up new camps, building boats, and selling fish.

9. *Success* was the boat that helped T. A. Bass to start the catfish business on Lake Okeechobee. Photo used by permission of the Florida Photographic Archives.

In November of 1911, he was shipping two carloads a week to Ft. Myers; he was employing seventy men and he owned sixteen boats. Of course, others were starting camps too, but before many years Captain Bass owned or furnished backing for a good share of all the camps on the lake. His son Lloyd says that Captain Bass owned no less than forty-five boats, eight refrigerated railroad cars, and no telling how many camps and nets. He didn't confine himself to fishing either, but branched out into other maritime activities. As early as 1913 he was hauling sand from Ft. Lauderdale's beach to be used in construction work.

Tom's glass cabin boat, *Echo,* towed construction material for building artificial islands in Biscayne Bay. In 1915, he got a contract to carry mail to Palm Beach and to Moore Haven. For this he used the steamer *Observation.* He used an old 64-foot tunnel-stern boat, the *Le Haven,* and Captain Hall's old *Corona* for hauling freight on Lake Okeechobee (Will, 117–118).

The first few years of catfishing were a boom time. Demand was good, the price held up, more camps were started, there was no lack of fish, and everybody was making good money. Captain Thomas A. Bass was flying high, but it was too good to last. Too many seines, no closed season, and the lowering of the lake combined to make catfish scarce. Bass refused to trim his operations and advanced money to distressed fishermen's families. He put money into camps when no one else would take the risk.

In 1917, fishing started to decline and both the Southern and Booth Fisheries moved their headquarters from Okeechobee to Jacksonville. Captain Tom entered into an agreement with F. M. Elledge of Standard Fish Company to receive $300,000.00 for 51 percent of his company and to stop fishing on Lake Okeechobee. One-third of the money was paid in cash, but Bass never got the remaining $200,000.

Bass tried buying fish again and in 1928 bought the Lakeside Fish Company in Pahokee. By this time catfishing was not like it used to be, and Captain Tom just couldn't survive. On January 25, 1935, Tom Bass died nearly broke (Will, 118–119).

I have tried to keep this history of steamboats on the Kissimmee as accurate as possible, but the material came from several books, papers, and notes that others had written years ago. Often the information was contradictory, but I have sorted it out as well as I could. If you read all the material I have included in the notes section of this book, you will understand what I mean. I believe, however, that the information I have furnished here is the most accurate account of steamboat activity on the Kissimmee to be found in one place.

4

Steamboats on the St. Johns

The mighty St. Johns River winds for 312 miles from Jacksonville to its southernmost point. The river flows from south to north, unlike most others. It begins in a flat marsh west of Vero Beach and then meanders slowly northward toward Jacksonville. It is the longest river in Florida.

The watershed of the river includes all or parts of sixteen counties in central and northwestern Florida. It is listed as one of fourteen American Heritage rivers in the United States and has inspired the literary works of Marjorie Kinnan Rawlings, Harriet Beecher Stowe, and others. The river's natural beauty attracted botanist John Bartram and artist James Audubon in their time. Today, development pressures, polluted storm water runoff, discharge from industrial waste, power facilities, and wastewater treatment plants have heavily impacted the St. Johns. Like most of America's large rivers, the health of the St. Johns is in question.

When the steamboats ran the river, it was considered pristine and one-of-a-kind in the world. More steamboat activity occurred here than in all the rest of Florida. On May 4, 1839, the *St. Augustine News* had the following comments by Major Henry Whiting, who visited the St. Johns in 1838: "The River (St. Johns) is in most respects of a thriving character. It is unlike most if not all of the rivers in North America, having little current at any point of its course, and passing through a country, from its very source, so level in its surface, as scarcely to warrant the expectation of any stream at all."

We will show a timeline here to describe steamboat activity on the St. Johns from the start to the end of the era.

1829–1835: The early beginnings of activity on the river. Not much known about this time period.
1835–1842: The second Seminole Indian War taking place with most of the steamboat activity by the military.
1842–1850: Regular passenger service begun, with a lot of shipbuilding activity and local travel.
1850–1861: Regular service from Charleston and Savannah. Local service is on the increase.
1862–1865: Travel almost at a standstill because of the Civil War.
1865–1875: Reconstruction and the reestablishment of old travel patterns.
1875–1887: The golden age of travel on the river.
1887–1890s: Gradual decline because of railroads and freezes. (Mueller, *Steamboating,* 9)

The first steamboat to reach Florida's east coast was the *George Washington.* It arrived on May 18 or 19, 1829, while on an excursion from Savannah. The boat was built in 1827 at Charleston and is alleged to have reached Jacksonville on the St. Johns. Jacksonville was at that time only a little settlement (11). Sporadic passages to the St. Johns were made by vessels from Savannah such as the *George Washington* for the first few years of the 1830s. Starting in 1834, the steamboat *Florida* ran until the end of the decade (11).

The second Seminole Indian War saw stepped-up activity on the St. Johns. Many of the logistical problems of the military were best served by water.

After the war small settlements along the river had regular service resumed. This service was often on a more than once a week basis (Mueller, *Steamboating,* 11).

Local service on the St. Johns commenced in the 1840s. The *Sarah Spalding* began service to Mellonville (now part of Sanford) and Enterprise. Jacob Brock's *Darlington* was on the St. Johns in the early 1950s to provide service as far as Lake Monroe. Another steamer, the *Hancock,* also ran from Jacksonville to Enterprise (11).

Direct service to the St. Johns was started in 1851 by the 350-ton *Florida.* This boat was built in New York and was quite successful. The direct service was from Charleston through Savannah and on to Jacksonville.

In 1852, the *Carolina,* which was a much bigger vessel, joined the *Florida* on the run. Two other boats made their appearance in 1852. They were the *St. Johns* and the *Seminole.* They ran for only a short time. Both of these boats burned while moored in Jacksonville within seven months of each other (11). Competition and business continued to increase until the Civil War; but after the war started, the Federal blockade soon cut all service. A lot of the Florida-bound vessels became blockade runners for the Confederacy and some were lost. A few returned later to resume their old runs.

After the war, business returned as usual and began to build. Some of the old boats returned and were joined by a host of new ones.

The real "boom" days came to the river after 1875. The DeBary-Baya Merchants Line emerged as the chief fleet on the river. Other passenger and freight services also came into being during this time. The first seven years of the 1880s were the high point of traffic on the river (12).

After the 1880s, the boom days were over because of the railroads, freezes, and changes to the harbor. Large coastal steamers reduced the steamboats' role to local use and catering to tourists who were coming to the state in large numbers. Even this business soon evaporated. The workboat fleets continued to operate for a number of years but eventually lost out to gasoline- and diesel-powered craft (Mueller, *Steamboating,* 12).

The boats that ran the river when the steamboat era began could be classified as coastal steamers, river steamers, and shallow draft vessels for restricted waters, like ferries, towboats, and packets. The packets carried mail, passengers, and freight. Packets were also classified as either night boats or day boats and by their means of propulsion. The side-wheeler was the most often used on the St. Johns although there were others that had a stern wheel or propeller. We also find there was a classification as to design of the boats. They were either called Eastern or Western type vessels. An Eastern steamboat design generally had one or two decks with fairly luxurious passenger accommodations. They were generally side-wheel boats. They also had the ability to carry some freight and most often had a shapely and graceful appearance.

Steamboats built in the Midwest or in the South had a more boxy shape, one or two decks, and sparse passenger accommodations. They were more likely to be stern-wheel boats. Boats that were built to travel the Mississippi and Ohio rivers and some others were true Western river steamboats. They were much larger in size than the Midwestern and Southern boats and had good accommodations for the passengers. They were like the Eastern steamboats in most ways (10).

Savannah, Georgia, and Charleston, South Carolina, were the major Southern seaports on the east coast and were served by large Northern boats and some boats that originated in Europe. They were also the ports most often used for passengers and freight that were going to Florida, Savannah being the best-established port.

Passengers and freight that arrived from the north on large boats had to be transferred to smaller ones for the Florida trip. The reason was the shallow water at the mouth of the St. Johns River. This "bar," as it was called, only allowed vessels with a draft of 6 to 8 feet to enter the mouth of the river. Almost all bodies of water in Florida that had their entrances from the sea had these bars, and some could be entered only under ideal conditions.

After a ship was inside the bar on the St. Johns, it followed a torturous channel, but the water was generally deep enough for passage (10).

Southern-built vessels were mostly used along the eastern seacoast in the 1820s when most steamboating began on the St. Johns River. Part of the reason was that the technology of the day used lower steam pressure and developed only modest horsepower. Another reason was that boats could be repaired by almost any blacksmith or handyman. The engine was placed in the middle of the boat and used side wheels for propulsion. This gave the boats better balance and provided more passenger comfort. The boats were mostly shallow draft vessels that could run reliably in the state's waters. Very large boats were never used much on the St. Johns. Most of the passenger boats used for local service were only 60 to 80 feet in length (Mueller, *Steamboating*, 10).

Two steamboats that saw service during the Civil War were the *Dictator* and the *City Point*. They were almost look-a-like vessels although they had been built a year apart and in different locations.

The *City Point* was built in 1864 by George Greenman, whose family shipyard is today the site of Mystic Seaport at Mystic, Connecticut. Some famed clipper ships had been built there as well as some well-built steamboats.

The *City Point* was a wooden, side-wheel vessel of 678 gross and 578 net tons. The boat was 204 feet long with a width of 31 feet and a draft of 7 feet. The 7-foot draft made her a good boat for crossing the shallow bar at Jacksonville. The engine was a vertical beam Fulton Iron Works product that had a cylinder of 45 inches in diameter and a stroke of 132 inches. She originally had a large tubular boiler in her hold (Mueller, *St. Johns*, 7).

The *Dictator* was built in 1863 by Thomas Stark in Williamsburg, New York. *Dictator* was of 735 gross tons and her dimensions were 205.5 feet long by 30 feet wide with a draft of 8.6 feet. Her engine was also a Fulton Iron Works but had a cylinder of 44 inches and a stroke of 132 inches.

The *City Point's* career started when she was chartered by the U.S. government in 1864 at a rate of $450 a day. This charter lasted until May of 1865. The vessel operated on the James River in Virginia carrying troops and supplies for General Ulysses S. Grant. When her military career was over, she ran for a few months between Richmond and Norfolk on the James River.

The *Dictator* was called *Conquest* when she was launched, but on her first passage her name was *Dictator* (7). This trip was from New York to New Orleans in 1863.

The ship was later chartered by the U.S. Army Quartermaster Department at a rate of $350 per day and until May 7, 1865. The end of hostilities brought an end to the charter (8).

The first few months after the war, both *City Point* and *Dictator* ran between Norfolk and Richmond after peacetime navigation was restored on the James River. George Leary partnered with William J. Pease and George Greenman to test the winter tourist trade in Florida. Leary was part of the famous Leary Steamship Line and Pease was from New York. George Greenman was from the Mystic, Connecticut, shipyard mentioned earlier. They established a run from Charleston to Jacksonville and then on to Palatka, Florida. By the fall of 1865, the *City Point* was in place for the regular service between Charleston and Florida. She arrived in Florida for the first time on November 20, 1865 (8).

On December 26, 1865, the *City Point* picked up an additional owner who was also her master. He was Captain E. C. Talbot, who was living in Charleston at the time. He knew the coastal waters well and was a well-known captain. The initial purser on the *City Point* was D. L. Bill. His job was to see to the 150 passengers when the vessel was running at capacity (8).

The *City Point* was very successful on the run from Charleston, Savannah, Fernandina, Jacksonville, Hibernia, Magnolia, Green Cove Springs, and Palatka. She also stopped at all the way landings on the St. Johns. Her first passage arrived at Jacksonville on November 23 or 24 of 1865. She was the largest vessel ever to come to Jacksonville in commercial service. The first trip was made in twenty-four hours from Charleston to Savannah and seventeen hours from Savannah to Jacksonville. The winter tourist season proved to be a good one, so in March of 1866 the *Dictator* joined the run with *City Point* (9).

The *Dictator* made her first appearance in Jacksonville on March 22, 1866, with her Captain Louis Mitchell Coxetter as master. He was a veteran of the Charleston to Florida trade and had pioneered the service in the early 1850s. He also was a very successful blockade runner for the Confederacy during the war. Coxetter was the master of the most successful Confederate privateer *Jeff Davis*.

For several years both boats were used for the winter tourist season, and one boat would go to New York for the summer. Periodically the vessels were overhauled after their summer's work, usually in New York. Occasionally both boats would run all summer to Florida and get minor repairs and overhaul accomplished at Charleston (Mueller, *St. Johns*, 10).

During the 1866 to 1867 winter season *Dictator* would leave Charleston at 10 p.m. on Friday and arrive in Savannah the next morning. She would then leave at 3 p.m. for Florida. She would leave Jacksonville on Monday morning to Palatka and then return the same day. The return trip to Savannah began at the unearthly hour of 3 a.m. on Tuesday. The boat arrived in Savannah on Wednesday morning. The final leg to Charleston was made by that evening (10).

For the 1867 to 1868 season the master of the *City Point* was Simpson Adkins. He was a veteran pilot-navigator from Charleston and had also been involved in the Civil War as a blockade runner.

In the summer of 1868 *Dictator* was substantially overhauled and returned to the Florida service. Upon her return in September to Jacksonville she was in every respect a first-class boat in fine order, her engine overhauled and put in good condition, her staterooms renovated and painted. Captain Coxetter was well known to the traveling public, and his newly refurbished boat would be just as popular.

October of 1868 saw the *City Point* with a new master, Captain William McNelty. October was also a month of tragedy for this vessel. While at Tybee at the mouth of the Savannah River, she anchored to wait for the tide to turn. When she was ready to get under way again the new Second Mate, James Patey, got his leg caught in a coil of the anchor cable. When the anchor was taken up, the leg was badly mangled. Patey died shortly after from loss of blood (11).

In May of 1872, the *Dictator* was given an inspection at Charleston. After this, she embarked on a trip to St. Augustine and had the misfortune to run aground. The passengers had become bored and impatient by the time the *Dictator* was freed.

In 1873, the *Dictator* and the *City Point* were both running the route, but a tragedy occurred on the *Dictator* in May when a deckhand fell overboard and was struck by one of the paddle wheels, thereby damaging it. It was announced that the *Dictator* was going off her route and steaming north for repairs.

For the 1873 to 1874 winter season, the *Dictator* and the *City Point* both ran the route to Florida and made a round trip every week, arriving at Jacksonville on Mondays and Thursdays. Palatka was still their upriver terminal. Captain Leopold Vogel was now master of the *Dictator*. The popular Captain Coxetter had died that summer in Charleston. Vogel was a man who would go on to command some of the largest and finest vessels ever to grace the St. Johns.

The *City Point* and *Dictator* were both overhauled and refitted in the summer of 1874, and the *Dictator* came back on the route in July. The ship's officers now wore blue uniforms. A small brass cannon had been placed on board and was used to mark arrivals and departures (12–13).

During the 1876 to 1877 season, the *Dictator* continued to be captained by Leo Vogel. R. F. Scott was the new master of the *City Point*. Both boats were making one round trip a week, and the railroads now made connection at Fernandina, Jacksonville, and Tocoi. At Palatka connections were now being made for the upper St. Johns River steamboats and the Ocklawaha River boats (Mueller, *St. Johns*, 12).

By the 1877 to 1888 winter season, the *City Point* and *Dictator* were both showing their age and becoming expensive to operate. A new vessel was being built by Charles Leary to take their place. This boat was the *St. Johns* and carried the number 115633. She was 250 feet long and had a speed of 19.5 miles per hour. Her speed allowed the boat to make two trips a week when needed (13).

The *Dictator* stayed on until the end of the 1889 to 1880 season as a spare boat. The *City Point* went north and was finally lost when she went aground on Plum Island near Newburyport, Massachusetts.

After the 1879 to 1880 season, the *Dictator* was reported sold to parties in New York, where she became a freighter (15). This marked the end for two great steamboats that had figured so prominently in establishing the route from Charleston to Palatka and back. They had seen many years of faithful service on the coastal waters and rivers of Florida.

The *St. Johns* began life in 1878 at the Wilmington, Delaware, firm of Harlan and Hollingsworth. She was launched on August 27, 1878, and hurriedly finished so she could take her place in the winter tourist business from Charleston to Palatka (17). The boat was iron hulled with two masts. *St. Johns* was 250 feet long and 38 feet wide except at her paddle wheel where she was 64 feet wide. The depth of the vessel's hull was 12.5 feet to the water. The engine was vertical beam and had a piston of 66 inches in diameter and a stroke of 12 feet. The ship had three boilers, each 22.5 feet long and 125 inches in diameter. The engine produced 1500 horsepower and pushed her through the water at almost twenty miles an hour. She had a gross ton capacity of 1,098 and 677 net tons.

The *St. Johns* was designed to do the jobs of two others—to make two runs to Charleston and back every week. That is what the *St. Johns* accomplished. She had to make the runs and remain virtually trouble free and be turned around quickly at the end of the runs. Her first season from 1878 to 1879 proved the boat could do it. In the slow summer seasons she was sent back north for the excursion season there.

The initial owner of *St. Johns* was the Commercial Navigation Company of Charleston. Charles Leary was president of the company. In Florida it was called "Charleston, Savannah and Florida Steamship Company" (Mueller, *St. Johns*, 18).

The *St. Johns* served the Florida trade well until she finished her winter season in 1881 and 1882. The *Jacksonville Times Union* on April 29, 1882 announced:

> Her Last Trip-The magnificent steamer *St. Johns* has made her last trip this season to this city, and it may be the last time she will ever be seen in our waters, and it may be many years before we will again see her equal here. There has probably been no boat in America that has accomplished more than the *St. Johns* since she made her first trip here. The gigantic fact of two round trips per week from Charleston to Palatka, calling in at Savannah and Fernandina both ways, making eight landings on the St. Johns River every trip, and loading seventy-five cords of wood each trip, besides her freight each way,

> which has always been large, is a wonder in steam boating when we know that the distance made by her to accomplish this is fourteen hundred miles per week. The New York Herald, in speaking of this splendid steamer, when she was fitting up in that city, before she came south, said she was the fastest boat that ever tied to a New York pier. Her performance at sea as a sea-going vessel has been grand and has astonished many. She has been the pride of Jacksonville and the St. Johns River, a great favorite with the traveling public, and admired by everyone for her perfect discipline and beauty. We will all miss her very much. (Mueller, *St. Johns*, 19–20)

After leaving Jacksonville she was sent back north and sold by the Learys for $110,000 to the New Jersey Southern Steamboat Company. The ship had an illustrious career in the North serving with different companies and in many different roles (21).

In 1927, forty-nine years after the *St. Johns* was built, she was sold again and rebuilt extensively at the Sparrows Point, Maryland, shipyard of the Bethlehem Steel Company. The ship was converted to an oil burner with a capacity of 29,000 gallons that gave her a range of 2,160 miles. An entirely new superstructure was added, giving her a rather boxy, angular, and altogether clumsy appearance. The new additions also reduced her speed to perhaps thirteen miles an hour. The vessel's name was changed to *Bombay.*

On June 12, 1931, the name was again changed to *Tolchester* and the boat was used to make two trips a day from Tolchester Beach to Baltimore, Maryland (24).

In 1941, the *Tolchester* was at her Baltimore pier when a fire broke out and turned into a six-alarm affair. *Tolchester* and another ship were towed away from the pier into the harbor while firefighters fought the pier fire. When the flames were extinguished, *Tolchester* had extensive damage. In November of 1941, *Tolchester* was towed to the Key Highway shipyard of Maryland Steel and Dry Dock Company and her hull was made into a barge.

In December of 1964, the old ship's registration was finally dropped and her life afloat came to an end. Her hull was finally used in a harbor landfill project. *St. Johns*, the pride of the Charleston, Savannah, Steam Packet Company, lasted a long time and served faithfully during it all (26–27).

Steamboat races were something that occurred on all the major rivers of the United States from time to time. The one most remembered by people who study the old boats was the race between the *Natchez* and the *Robert E. Lee.* The boats raced from New Orleans to St. Louis on the Mississippi River in 1870, and arguments still go on today as to which boat won. Steamboat captains and owners took great pride in their vessels. To prove which had the fastest boat, they would sometimes have such a race. They thought it would impress the passengers and perhaps it satisfied some egos.

A race also took place on the St. Johns River that is all but forgotten today between the *H. T. Baya* and the *John Sylvester*. Rivalry on the river was at a height a few years before the railroads began to dominate the winter visitor trade, and the steamship companies took every advantage to win passengers and freight for their individual enterprises.

The *H. T. Baya* was a brand new boat that arrived in Jacksonville in 1882. It had been recently commissioned by Hanaro T. Baya and named after him. The Baya line vessels were very prominent on the St. Johns at the time (Mueller, *St. Johns*, 70).

The *John Sylvester* was an older vessel owned by the Post Line and had been constructed in 1866 by the well-known Allison Works in New Jersey. She was built of wood and was 193 feet long, 30 feet wide and over 50 feet over her side-wheel box. The engine was constructed by Murphy,

10. Steamboat *Sylvester* loaded with passengers. Photo used by permission of the Florida Photographic Archives.

McCurdy, and Warden and was of the vertical beam type with a 44-inch cylinder and a 10-foot piston stroke. The ship was 495 gross tons and 338 tons net.

The *H. T. Baya* was about 12 feet longer than the Sylvester and had a lot more tonnage as well as more horsepower. By all rights, she should have been a much faster boat. Since she was new, however, she had not been fine-tuned and was not as limber as the *John Sylvester*.

The *John Sylvester* was a finely tuned steamboat and had a well-deserved reputation for speed. She was also a shallow draft vessel and more adaptable to the St. Johns River than the *Baya* (71).

Colonel Baya was a veteran of the Confederate cause and had a large amount of Southern pride. The Post families were ardent Northerners and were looked on as interlopers and newcomers to the area. The significance of the race was substantially more than one steamboat competing against another for supremacy on the river; it was North against South again. The chief source of information about this race is the *Jacksonville Union*'s account of it in the January 9, 1883, issue. On Monday, January 8, 1881, in the evening when the *H. T. Baya* and the *John Sylvester* pulled up at their nearby piers with their steam apparatus apparently exhausted, it was concluded by the unknown *Jacksonville Union* writer that "the most exciting race in the history of the St. Johns River has ended." It was indicated that "nothing in recollection ever stirred Jacksonville more than this long expected race between the two well known and popular steamers."

On Monday morning at 9 o'clock, these boats were cheered on by the thronging, shouting audience crowding most of the piers fringing the St. Johns. "The two racers of the river started out fresh, graceful and buoyant, nose to nose, each confident yet cautious cheer after cheer rent the air as the two steamers reached Grassy Point with no change in their relative positions." Apparently at that instant, "The *H. T. Baya* gained a slight advantage, which was greeted by cheers by its friends, but there was scarcely a noticeable difference between the two vessels. The two splendid vessels settled themselves squarely down to the stern uncertain struggle and thus went out of sight, their sterns parallel and their walking beams keeping time, side by side." Those at the crowded docks were still cheering them on even as they rounded the curve of the St. Johns at Point La Vista. By the time the vessels had arrived at Remington Park, the *H. T. Baya* was about a half-length ahead. At that point, the *John Sylvester* came up alongside and laid her wheel rather "affectionately," as the writer put it, "alongside the wheel house of the *Baya* and in this familiar fashion the twain proceeded as bosom friends with locked arms to the buoy at Green Cove Springs, turned sharply there and headed for the dock with not a ray of daylight showing between their sides and their passengers shaking hands across the guards of the rival-welded steamers." As the unknown writer described it, "This was the most exciting part of this most exciting race." If the boats had kept their straight course, as it appeared they would do, they would have knocked the dock and the people into the river. Each boat was trying desperately for advantage here. The *Baya* on the right hoped to crowd the *Sylvester* off to the left of the dock and take possession. The *Sylvester*, however, threw her guards above the *Baya* and gave her rudder a sudden turn to starboard, throwing the *Baya* off the dock to shoreward and thus taking the dock. Obviously the *H. T. Baya* had been out-maneuvered at this point, but she countered by quickly throwing her mailbags ashore and backed out without actually making the landing and was a clear one-half mile ahead by the time her rival was leaving the dock. It should be pointed out that the *H. T. Baya* had her sides above her guards and forward of her wheel on the port side bashed in during the side-to-side "locked together procession" of the two boats between Remington and Green Cove Springs. The *John Sylvester*'s starboard guard had been elevated by moving the passengers and the chain box to the port side, thus raising her heavy guard and then smashing it into the *H. T. Baya*'s framework as the passengers went to the other side and the chain boxes were moved to the starboard side.

After leaving Green Cove Springs and proceeding to Tocoi, the *H. T. Baya* kept her lead and was leaving the Tocoi pier when the *John Sylvester* was arriving. The *H. T. Baya* reached the Palatka wharf at 1:29 p.m., only five minutes ahead of the *John Sylvester*. At Palatka, it was found that the minuscule supply of coal put on board the *H. T. Baya* at Jacksonville had given out and accordingly, she had a maddening wait until she had replenished her bunkers.

Meanwhile, the *John Sylvester*, which had fallen behind at Green Cove Springs, came up and in turn docked at Palatka. She then started the return trip to Jacksonville ahead of the *H. T. Baya* by several miles. At the Green Cove Springs landing, however, the *H. T. Baya* did not go in and consequently got ahead of the *John Sylvester*, which made the landing. The *H. T. Baya*, because of this strategy, led by four lengths and maintained this lead until she came in ahead by the same margin in Jacksonville at the finish of the race.

The end of the race was filled with controversy, each boat thinking the other had won. Their supporters had the same opinions. The upshot of it all is that neither boat won the race and they both knew it. Some thought they should have another race to Palatka and back without stopping, but then a lot of people declared, "As exciting as the race may be it is to a large degree dangerous and improper" (Mueller, *St. Johns*, 72–75).

Napoleon Bonaparte Broward was a famous governor of Florida who owned a steamboat and used it on and around the St. Johns. In fact, he and his brother Montcalm and George DeCottes raised $40,000 to build a powerful oceangoing tug to be used for towing and wrecking along the south Florida reefs. They also planned to carry freight and passengers between Jacksonville and Nassau in the Bahamas. The Broward brothers had grown up along the St. Johns and were very familiar with the river and all the various enterprises that had arisen near it through the years.

The name of the boat was the *Three Friends* and signified the triple ownership of the vessel. The name had been determined by an auction that decided the name of the boat by selling the privilege of naming her to the highest bidder. The winner was George DeCottes who bid $80, and he named the new boat.

The fastest tug in the South at the time was the *Dauntless*, but the new *Three Friends* was expected to be even faster (Procter, 97). The *Three Friends* was built by J. Daly and Charles Scammel who owned a boatbuilding business on Fort George Island, Florida. She was to be 125 feet long, and 23 feet wide with a hold 10 feet deep amidships, 12 feet deep forward, and 13 feet deep from heel to deck at the stern. Napoleon Broward designed the boat himself and whittled out the hull shape. The designated wood materials consisted of live oak for the stern apron and stern post, white pine for deck planks, and yellow pine for the main keelson, which was a 12 x 12-inch timber. A unique wood called Madeira that came from Andros Island in the Bahamas was used for the knees and frame material. The yellow pine hull planking was of varying thicknesses: three, two, and one-half inches. Most of the remainder of the wood used was yellow pine. The engines for the boat came from the Jacksonville Machine and Iron Works, which was part of Merrill-Stevens, later to become Jacksonville Shipyards—said to be one of the best in the country. The engines rated at 505 horsepower and were of the triple-expansion type with three cylinders of 14-, 21-, and 25-inch diameters. Each one had a 24-inch piston stroke. The fuel used for the boat was coal.

11. The *Three Friends* was a steamboat owned by former governor Napoleon Bonaparte Broward and used in a war with Cuba. Photo used by permission of the Florida Photographic Archives.

The vessel was finally launched on February 2, 1895, and christened *Three Friends* by Hortense Broward who was Napoleon's younger sister (116–117).

The *Three Friends* was on the threshold of finding a place in history as newspapers on February 28, 1895, announced that an insurrection had broken out between Spain and Cuba and that Spanish authority on the island was falling apart. Spanish officials assured the world the incident was unimportant, but Cubans along the Atlantic coast received the news with great interest. The Cuban provinces of Matanzas and Santiago de Cuba were under martial law, and American newspapers filled front pages with startling headlines. A new chapter in history was beginning for America and Cuba.

"Cuba Libra" was the cry of the day, and Cuban revolutionists capitalized on American sympathy. Anything to do with the ideals of liberty and democracy always inspired American interest.

In the 1800s, a filibuster was known as a person who unlawfully initiated or supported revolts against South and Central American governments in order to enrich himself.

The Cubans on the island were in dire need of supplies of all kinds, and revolutionists wanted to use the United States as their base for filibustering expeditions to their army. The vigilance of U.S. authorities kept two-thirds of the supplies from reaching their destinations. Spain never appreciated these efforts. Grover Cleveland was president of the United States at the time and said aid would not come from the government and that if any did, it would be through private capital.

Florida's long coastline and her proximity to Cuba made the state a filibuster's haven. There were so many places to hide that a ship could easily slip out and make the trip to Cuba undetected (Procter, 98).

Many Cubans were living in the lower Florida Keys and some on the other islands in the Keys. There was also a large Cuban colony in Jacksonville where the *Three Friends* was being built.

That summer, while *Three Friends* was being completed, a junta from Jacksonville approached Broward at various times concerning the possibility that his new boat could be used to help Cuba. The junta had been organized by J. A. Huau, a successful cigar manufacturer in Jacksonville and also a close friend to Broward. Huau's store served as a secret meeting place for the revolutionaries.

Broward knew what the government's stand was on those who helped the insurgents, but he viewed the insurrection as simply a case of an oppressed people rising to free itself from alien tyranny (98). He wanted to help the Cubans and decided that if he did he would stay within the law. He would agree to transport patriots only if they would sign the ship's log as passengers. He would not take munitions unless they were carried beyond the three-mile limit by another vessel and then loaded on the *Three Friends*. He felt that technically such transactions would not violate the law (100).

Napoleon Broward eventually became involved in filibustering actions to help the Cubans and made many trips to and from Cuba with supplies of arms, munitions, and troops aboard the *Three Friends.* He was almost captured several times, and his vessel was boarded by U.S. inspection officials many times, but he was never caught. Broward and his vessel became heroes in the eyes of the people who read about his exploits, and this definitely helped him become governor of Florida in 1905 (Procter, 100–120).

It was natural that fathers wanted to pass on their knowledge and love of steamboats to their sons, and there were several father-son combinations on the St. Johns during the era of the boats. One was T. Walker Lunds and his son. Another was Jacob Brock and his son Charles, whom I covered in chapter 1. For many decades the father-son duo of H. D. DeGrove and his son Henry D. Jr. would run the St. Johns and capture their share of the business and commerce along the river.

The DeGrove family came to Florida from Louisville, Kentucky, in 1874 and settled in Fruit Cove along the St. Johns. The patrician of the family was William Michael DeGrove, who had brought his family there largely because of a preacher who spoke at great length about the Sunshine State.

William had operated a telegraph office in Louisville before he came to Florida. One of his workers at the office liked to dabble with chemicals. On one occasion the employee tipped over some chemicals that leaked through the floor to the one below and ruined Mr. DeGrove's carpet. The worker was promptly fired and went on to fame as probably the greatest inventor and scientist of all time. His name was Thomas Alva Edison.

The Florida freezes of 1879–1880 almost wiped out the family fortunes; also, William and his wife died in 1881. The children had to go to work at an early age to survive. One of William's ten children got his first job feeding wood to the furnaces of steamboats. He was Henry DeGrove Sr. Henry rapidly progressed and served some time on the DeBary-Baya Line, which was then the premier line on the river. He became licensed as a helmsman in May of 1882 when he was only twenty-two years old. He became licensed as a second-class pilot nine months after that. Henry obtained his first-class license a year later and rose to master pilot in 1885. Henry Sr. stayed on the river most of his life, except in his middle years when he went into retail merchandising and contracting.

In December of 1886, Henry switched from the DeBary-Baya Line to the Beach and Miller Line. A year later he was on the *Manatee* from Tampa Bay and also served on the *Crescent City* as purser when she replaced the *Manatee.* After his service with the Beach and Miller Line, Henry spent the remainder of his service on the river with the Garner steamboating interests (Mueller, *St. Johns*, 40).

Captain Charles Edward Garner migrated to Florida in 1881 and started his steamboat line with the *Port Royal*. His interest was chiefly with local traffic on the lower St. Johns. His father was involved with several steamboat lines up north and had been master of several vessels. That had a lot to do with his son's interest.

Charles had other business interests besides steamboats. He was involved with the South Jacksonville Water Works Company and was director of three other companies. He helped establish the Florida National Bank of Jacksonville and was the bank's first president. In 1913, he stepped up to chairman of the board. He was also president of the Florida Bank and Trust Company. Garner held many prestigious positions in the Jacksonville community over the years until he died in 1915. After his death, Henry DeGrove Sr. became president and general manager of Garner's Independent Line. DeGrove had a considerable financial interest in this line and had been vice-president in 1912 (143). In the mid-1910s and early 1920s, the Independent Line was flourishing and Henry DeGrove Jr. became active in it along with his father. He also had an early interest in steamboats and began working for his father as a teenager. His first assignment was quartermaster on the *May Garner*, which was named after Captain Garner's daughter. After three years, his father gave him command of the *Keystone*. Ten years later Henry Jr. became master of the *Magnolia* (147).

The *May Garner* was initially intended as a tug, but instead she was used to carry mail, passengers, and freight. The boat was 94.3 feet long by 26 feet wide with a hold of 6.6 feet and built of native yellow pine. The vessel had two state rooms, three berths, and was licensed for seventy-six cabin and fifty deck passengers. The engine was a small condensing type of 16-inch cylinder diameter with a 1.5-foot stroke. The boiler was 12 feet long by 7 feet in diameter. She was a wood burner and carried a lot of cargo like livestock, bales of hay, groceries, and general supplies. The first car ever owned in Green Cove Springs was a yellow roadster that was delivered to the owner by the *May Garner*. The whole town turned out for the occasion (146).

The *Keystone* was acquired by the DeGroves in 1913. It was a trim little vessel that was built as a private yacht around 1893 for Mary Packer Cummings. She used the boat for service between downtown Jacksonville and Keystone Bluff which was her winter residence. The *Keystone* was named after her home state of Pennsylvania. She died in 1912, and the DeGroves bought the boat then.

The *Keystone* was 53.3 feet long by 11 feet wide and had a 5-foot draft. She had a triple-expansion condensing engine with an Almay water-tube boiler and used anthracite coal as fuel. There was also a steam electric plant on board (Mueller, *St. Johns*, 146–147).

The last vessel acquired by the DeGroves was the *Magnolia*. She was built in Jacksonville in 1917–1918 at the Anderson Dry Dock and Repair Yards. The vessel was built to conform to new rules that said vessels of 65 feet or less could employ a smaller crew than larger boats. She was 64 feet, 11 inches long by 22 feet wide and had a draft of 6 feet. The *Magnolia* had a fore and aft compound steam engine and an Almay water-tube boiler. In 1926, the steam engine was replaced by a 60 horsepower Fairbanks Morse oil engine.

All of the Independent Line's steamboats were driven by wooden propellers except the *Manatee*, which was an iron side-wheeler. They all ended their careers away from the St. Johns (147).

The *Mary Draper* was sold to J. S. Stevens of Edisto Island, South Carolina, and was placed on the mail run from Edisto Island.

The *May Garner* was sold to parties in Georgia and was destroyed by fire at Brunswick, Georgia, on July 10, 1921.

The *Keystone* was sold to a Jacksonville tug owner and captain in the 1920s. She was converted to a small tug and her old engine was replaced by a Fairbanks Morse 60 horsepower diesel.

DeGrove decided the steamboating era was at its end when he finally sold the *Magnolia* to parties in Georgia. The Independent Line was finished (148).

Henry Sr. was by now a contractor and owned Enterprise Grocery Company and Standard Concrete. He also owned the Jacksonville Water Works Company. The DeGrove family owned Pier #3 on the North River in New York City, which they sold in 1896. Henry Sr. retired in the early 1930s and died in 1951.

Captain Henry DeGrove Jr. continued to work on the river as much as he could after the steamboat line closed. In 1930 and 1931 he was master of the excursion boat *Utility*. After that, he was master and pilot for the Florida Ferry Company. They operated a ferry service between downtown Jacksonville and the south side of the river. The vessels he served were the double-enders *Fletcher* and *Jackson*.

For a time DeGrove was the master of a private yacht that belonged to the Mead paper family. He sailed the yacht to Connecticut, Massachusetts, Maine, the Great Lakes, and Washington, D.C. His wife Clara sometimes worked on the yacht as the cook. While he was with the Meads, he was also master of a tug that towed wartime petroleum barges on the Intracoastal Waterway and the St. Johns.

After service with the Meads and the wartime tugs, DeGrove was associated with the Huckins Yacht Corporation and delivered many yachts to their new owners. He saw many of them through their shakedown cruises. When the Buccaneer toll road was built after World War II, it left a water gap from Fernandina Beach to Jacksonville Beach, and the Ft. George-Mayport Ferry Company started. DeGrove became one of the first captains on the double-ender *Jean Lafitte.* He later served as master of the *Buccaneer* and the *Blackbeard.* As of 1985, both these boats were still in service.

Henry DeGrove Jr. served on the river for over sixty years as a boy and a man. He died in November 1972 and was laid to rest alongside his father in the old Mandarin cemetery. He was the last of the steamboat captains of old on the St. Johns (Mueller, *St. Johns,* 148–151).

Another father-son team on the St. Johns was Frederick DeBary and his son Adolph. Samuel Frederick DeBary was born in Frankfurt, Germany, on January 15, 1814, and was a descendant of Belgian royalty, which gave him the title of Count. His son was born in 1845.

Frederick's two younger brothers were in the champagne-producing business in France, and Frederick was given the exclusive franchise to distribute the company's products in the United States. In 1851, he and his family moved there and established homes in Summit, New Jersey, and New York. DeBary also established an elaborate winter home just south of what is now DeBary, Florida, near the St. Johns River and Lake Monroe (Mueller, *Steamboating,* 81).

After the Civil War, DeBary spent much of his time in his Florida home and developed the 400 acres into a plantation that grew sugarcane and had a grits mill. The property was planted in citrus, camphor, bamboo, and other exotic shrubs and plants. His house was a two-story creation, the lower floor having a fifteen-foot ceiling, a large center hall, game room, parlor, library, master bedroom, kitchen, and servants' quarters. The second floor featured seven bedrooms and servants' quarters. A two-story verandah surrounded three sides of the wooden house. The house contained 8,000 square feet of living space.

The house and grounds has successfully withstood the ravages of time and can be visited today. The state of Florida owns it and has designated it a historic site.

DeBary's interest in steamboats began in March 1876 when he purchased the *George M. Bird*. The steamboat was small but could accommodate his many guests who visited the plantation for hunting parties. DeBary was known to love a party of any kind and always served his guests the famed wines and champagnes from his franchise. There was also plenty of food on hand, such as quail, venison, bear, and bass. Sometimes a steer was barbequed.

DeBary found that public transportation was needed on the St. Johns, so cabins were added to the somewhat sparse *George M. Bird*, and she catered to the tourist trade. The boat was built in New Bedford, Massachusetts, in 1871. In October of that year she was listed as being of 91.44 tons and 99.8 feet long. The boat was 22.65 feet wide and had a draft of 4.68 feet. There was only one deck and no figurehead or masts. The vessel was a sternwheeler. The *George M. Bird* operated in New Bedford until 1876 and was sold to Frederick DeBary on March 30, 1876. Sometime in 1876 she was lengthened at Jacksonville to 107 feet and her tonnage increased to 142 gross tons, 121 net. The listed horsepower was 150. Passenger accommodations and another deck were added (82–83).

Because of the tourist market, the *George M. Bird* was placed in regular service in 1877 and was on a run from Jacksonville to Sanford, Tocoi, Palatka, Enterprise, and Mellon Ville. She ran twice a week under Captain R. H. Stewart.

When the war started in 1861, the *George M. Bird* was placed under Confederate control and renamed *Governor Milton* after Florida's wartime governor.

In 1883 the *George M. Bird* was involved in a steamboat race on the St. Johns. As the boat was preparing to leave Sanford for Jacksonville, her captain, William Hallowes, received a challenge from Captain James W. Fitzgerald on the *H. B. Plant* that the *Plant* would beat him to Jacksonville. Hallowes accepted the challenge and left Sanford at full speed for Jacksonville. The African American pilot on the *Bird* went around the curves in the river at full speed even though it was customary to slow down for them because of shallow water. The boat did not slow down until she reached Jacksonville, well ahead of the *H. B. Plant* (Mueller, *Steamboating*, 83).

Since the steamboat business was so good, DeBary decided to expand and bought a second vessel named the *Rosa*. The boat was built in Wilmington, Delaware, in 1870 and was an iron-hulled side-wheeler. She was 136 feet long, 22 feet wide and had a draft of 5 feet. She carried 156 gross tons and had two inclined engines with 16-inch cylinders and 5-foot piston stroke. There was one boiler 6 feet, 7 inches at the front, 18 feet in length, with a diameter of 5 feet, 6 inches.

The *Rosa* was run on the Savannah River under Captain I. N. Philpot for awhile before DeBary bought her.

In January 1881, DeBary incorporated his two vessels into a steamboat line that was known as the DeBary Merchants Line. It was registered in New York, and he was designated president.

The third addition to DeBary's fleet was the *Florence*. She had previously been owned by Jacob Brock and used on his steamboat line. DeBary bought the *Florence* in June of 1881. The vessel was built in Wilmington, Delaware, in 1869 as a vertical beam side-wheeler. *Florence* was 135 feet long by 24.4 feet wide with a draft of 5.8 feet. She was of 263 gross tons and 176 net. Two months after he bought her, DeBary changed the boat's name to *Anita* in honor of his granddaughter. She then joined *George M. Bird* and *Rosa* in service on the river.

A steamboat owner usually can't resist the temptation to name a vessel after himself, so Count DeBary commissioned Pusey and Jones to build the *Frederick DeBary* in 1881. She was an iron-hulled vessel with a side wheel, 145.5 feet long and 24.2 feet wide with a draft of 7.5 feet. She was 336 gross tons and 267.91 tons net. The boat had a 750 horsepower engine with a cylinder diameter of 36 inches and a 6-foot stroke. It was a vertical beam engine. The DeBary Merchants Line took her over officially on January 21, 1882.

The last vessel added to the DeBary line was probably the finest boat DeBary ever owned. It was the *City of Jacksonville*. This vessel was another Wilmington, Delaware, product that was acquired in 1882 and was constructed by Harlan and Hollingsworth. They were known for the many fine ships they had constructed of iron and steel.

The *City of Jacksonville* was 169 feet long, 52 feet wide at the paddle wheels and had a depth of hold of 8 feet. She had two inclined engines, one for each wheel, with a cylinder diameter of 30 inches and a 72-inch stroke for each one. There were thirty-eight staterooms and officers' quarters on the main deck. The rooms were fitted with fine carpet and featured marble

12. The *Frederick DeBary* was named after a famous steamboat man on the St. Johns River. She is shown here at dock in Jacksonville, Florida. Photo used by permission of the Florida Photographic Archives.

washstands and plate glass windows, and were finished in mahogany and yellow pine. Each stateroom had two berths, the upper one arranged on hinges so it could be turned up against the wall to allow more room for the passengers. The steamer had three decks and was allowed to carry 275 passengers. The boat was furnished with two freight spaces with cranes for hoisting the freight aboard. At the rear of the main deck was a dining room with six tables. It was furnished with fine carpet, cut glass, red and white globes on the lights, and polished brass chandeliers with nickel-plated reflectors. The walls featured mahogany and pine that had been gilded and decorated. The grand salon on the second deck was furnished with fine carpets and had large comfortable red plush chairs, handsome beveled

French plate mirrors in mahogany frames, red and white skylights, and chairs and tables. The *City of Jacksonville* was indeed a well-appointed boat and one of the finest ever to travel the St. Johns River (Mueller, *Steamboating*, 84–87).

The DeBary Line was northern based and Frederick DeBary was a stanch Northerner himself, but he was challenged by a staunch Southerner in the same steamboat business. They would later become partners by combining their two lines and would eventually see the end of the steamboat era together. The Southerner was Hanaro T. Baya, a descendant of an early Spanish family that settled in St. Augustine upon receiving a charter to lands there from the Spanish crown. Baya was born in 1839 and lived in Florida all his life. He began his business career in 1856 when he left St. Augustine and went into partnership with P. J. Porcher of Charleston. The business was known as P. J. Porcher and Baya and was a small auctioneering and brokerage firm.

In 1861, Baya became a clerk in the Confederate Army Subsistence Department. In 1862, he was appointed a captain with the title of Assistant Commissary of Subsistence and was assigned to the 8th Florida Regiment under General Finnegan at the battle of Olustee. In May of 1865, he was made a colonel and paroled at Lake City, Florida. From that day on, he was known as Colonel Baya.

Colonel Baya settled in Jacksonville and entered the grocery business. This business became increasingly successful because he provided supplies and provisions for the many steamers plying the St. Johns. In 1885, the business was grossing about $100,000 annually, which made Baya a rich man in those days.

Around 1874, a small steamer was brought from the North and put into local service. She served only a short time before catching fire and burning to the waterline. This steamboat was the *Gazelle*. Baya bought the boat and had her extensively rebuilt, adding a new salon. The *Gazelle* started service on the lower river downstream from Jacksonville visiting the smaller settlements there. After a time, steamboating lured Baya away from his grocery business.

Business was so good another steamer was needed, so Baya and a partner, Joseph Parsons, bought the *Water Lily* and added her to the line in July 1879 (Mueller, *Steamboating*, 89). She was built in 1873 at Jersey City, New Jersey. The boat was 117.7 feet long and 18 feet wide with a draft of 5.4 feet. Gross tons were 118. The boat was a two-decked side-wheeler and had served as a commuter and excursion vessel in the New York area. She was added to Baya's line in the summer of 1889. The next Baya vessel was the *Sylvan Glen,* which turned out to be one of his fastest boats. The *Sylvan Glen* could go 17.5 miles per hour. The vessel was bought from a New York firm that was getting out of the steamboat business because a new elevated railroad was due to start operating in the city. The firm deduced that it would put the steamboats out of business, so the owners were selling them.

The *Sylvan Glen* was of 350 tons and 153.5 feet long with a width of 27.5 feet and a draft of 8.3 feet. The engine had a 40-inch cylinder with an 8-foot stroke (90).

After an extremely good winter season in 1881–1882, Baya went north and bought not one but two more steamboats. One was the *Magnolia* and the other he commissioned to have built. It was the *H. T. Baya.* Baya had succumbed to the lure of having a boat named after him.

The *Magnolia* was originally the *I. N. Seymour* and had been built in October of 1861 as a tug and dispatch boat. She served during the Civil War in various capacities and was sent to the Washington Navy Yard in May 1865. On June 20, 1865, she was renamed the *Tulip* and joined the U.S. Lighthouse Service, where she remained for seventeen years.

On June 7, 1882, Matthew H. Gregory of Red Bank, New Jersey bought the *Tulip* and renamed her *Magnolia.* Twelve days later he sold the boat to Baya. Gregory was a steamboat broker and had bought the *Tulip* at a government auction.

Magnolia could carry 250 passengers and sleep twenty-two when she was remodeled by William E. Woodall. She was 126 feet long and 37 feet wide and grossed 186 tons. The engine was a condensing type with a 30-inch cylinder and a 6-foot stroke. The boiler was 14 feet long and 7 feet in diameter and would carry 40 pounds of steam pressure. The boat's upper salon was fifty-two feet long and carpeted. There was also a salon on the main deck aft. The boat ran about thirteen miles an hour (91).

The boat Baya had commissioned and named after himself was a 669 gross and 411 net ton side-wheeler built by B. G. Hillman in Philadelphia in 1881. She was 205 feet long by thirty-two feet wide with a draft of 9.2 feet. She had a beam engine by Neafie and Levy with a cylinder of 52 inches and a stroke of 10 feet. Two larger boilers carried 55 pounds of steam. The guaranteed speed was 18 miles an hour in still water. The machinery alone reportedly cost $40,000.

Baya's namesake proved to be his undoing because she was too large to efficiently make the turns in the river. After a short period of employment on the river, she returned to the East where she found a variety of employment (91).

Baya ran his vessels through most of the winter of 1882–1883, but in March 1883 he decided to combine his boats with those of the DeBary Merchants Line and a new colossus on the St. Johns resulted, the DeBary-Baya Merchants Line (Mueller, *Steamboating*, 92).

The steamboat business in the late 1800s was flourishing on the St. Johns. By 1876, the country had recovered sufficiently from the Civil War that visitors had started coming to Florida again and their numbers were increasing. The railroads had also begun to come to the state, and one of the principal routes was from Jacksonville to Sanford. The steamboats still had to fill the void to other places along the river.

Citrus once flourished along the lower St. Johns, but the freezes of the 1880s took care of most of that. While it lasted, however, the citrus attracted visitors and was also a cargo for the steamboats.

The DeBary-Baya merger was a curious one in that one owner was an ardent Northerner and the other an ardent Southerner, but they both had steamboat fever and a desire to dominate the river trade. In May of 1883, all the vessel transfers were made and all the documents in order for the line to officially begin. Though they were independent operators before that, Baya had dominated the route from Jacksonville to Palatka and DeBary had controlled the route from Palatka to Sanford. When the two merged, they truly dominated the river.

For several months after the merger the new line made necessary shifts and adjustments as needed. No new vessels were purchased, and they made do with what they had.

In December of 1883, the DeBary-Baya Line had a catastrophe. The *Frederick DeBary* caught fire and burned on December 3, 1883, and was taken north to be rebuilt. The winter season was just starting, and another vessel was needed to replace the one damaged by fire (93).

On December 9 the *Fannie Dugan* was purchased and quickly overhauled and placed on the river. The boat was built in Portsmouth, Ohio, in 1872 and was a typical Ohio River packet. She was built out of wood and was 165 feet long and 28 feet wide with a draft of 4.5 feet. Most of her life was spent on a trade route between Portsmouth and Pomeroy, Ohio. Since *Fannie Dugan* was almost twelve years old when the DeBary-Baya Line purchased her, she was already past her prime. As it turned out, she was to last only eighteen months with this line.

The winter season of 1883–1884 was an especially good one for the new line, so the owners began to think of expanding their fleet of vessels. On January 29, 1884, they announced plans to build two large freight boats. One was to be of wood and the other of iron construction.

Only one vessel would result from this optimism and it was the *Everglade.* She was a homely stern-wheeler that was built in Jacksonville in 1884. The boat was of 413 gross and 206 net tons and was 134 feet long by 37.3 feet wide. Her draft was 5.6 feet, and the boat had two engines with a 16-inch cylinder and a piston stroke of 5.5 feet. She would serve primarily for the freight business and continued with the line until March of 1900 (Mueller, *Steamboating,* 94).

Much more could be said about steamboats on the St. Johns. A whole book could be written about that river alone. Edward Mueller, a steamboat expert from Jacksonville, did just that back in the 1980s. His books are now out of print but can be found in some rare book stores. Much of the information I have written about the St. Johns is taken from Mueller. Complete information on his books is included in the bibliography.

Steamboats on the Ocklawaha

"Ocklawaha" has been spelled many ways through the years. The chief variants are "Oclawaha," "Oklawaha," "Ocklewaha," "Ochlawaha," and "Ockalewaha." The river was named for the Indian tribes who once lived there (Mitchell, 4). The headwaters of the Ocklawaha are about halfway between Orlando and Ocala in a cluster of lakes. The principal bodies are Lake Harris, Lake Dora, Lake Eustis, and Lake Griffin. They are all navigable and have a combined water area of several hundred miles. Some of the ports the steamboats used along the way were Leesburg, Okahumpka, Astula, Tavares, Eustis, Fort Mason, and Orange Bend. Okahumpka was considered the head of navigation. From Lake Griffin, some eighty-five miles below Okahumpka, the Ocklawaha flows northward as a tributary of the St. Johns River.

The country north of the lakes is a vast cypress swamp, punctuated with small lakes and hammocks. Winding through all this swampland, the Ocklawaha looks like a dark jugular vein. It is weirdly contorted and loops around, doubling distance and then redoubling it until a navigator soon gets lost. A description from 1897 says that the river has no banks except tree trunks rising from the water, which is deep and dark and often reflects strangely the dense forest that grows down to its very edge. Save for a few infrequent landings where a promontory of high land projects into the stream, the swamp is unbroken (Mitchell, 6).

The swamp begins at Cow Ford, about forty miles below Lake Griffin, beyond which the river flows through sixteen miles of wilderness to the mouth of Silver Springs run, which pours in from the west. The run divides the upper and lower Ocklawaha. Seven miles downstream is Grahamville, which was once the village of Osceola, named after the famous Seminole chief. Thirty-one miles farther is the mouth of Orange Creek, the Ocklawaha's main tributary and the landing place for the town of Orange Springs. Here, the river makes its one major change of direction, swinging more than ninety degrees to the right and flowing eastward for thirty-three more miles to its junction with the St. Johns opposite the town of Welaka. This point is twenty-five miles upstream from Palatka. At this point the river has traveled 160 miles even though the straight line distance is only thirty-nine miles from the Lake Griffin outlet (Mitchell, 6).

In December 1856, the scientist and writer Daniel Garrison Brinton was one of the first to visit the now-famous Silver Springs. He came that way on a pole barge and carefully recorded his findings in his 1859 book, *Notes on the Floridian Peninsula*. His notes reflect what Silver Springs was like back then and what a wonder it still is today when approached from the Ocklawaha: "For more than a week I had been tediously ascending this river in a pole-barge, wearied with the monotony of the dank and gloomy forest that everywhere shades its inky stream, when one bright morning a sharp turn brought us into the pellucid waters of Silver Spring Run. A few vigorous strokes and we had left behind us the cypress swamps and emerged into broad level savannas." Brinton had come to Silver Springs in a most painful trip up a gloomy and amazing river, climaxed by one of the most dramatic transitions from darkness to light that a traveler can make anywhere on this continent. Modern publicity and new modes of travel have produced a moderately strange contrast to the state of things just half a century away, when almost everyone in America had heard of "the dark and gloomy Ocklawaha" and "the wonderfully clear Silver Spring Run" (Mitchell, 4).

There were no steamboats on the river when Daniel Brinton published his book. The region was very sparsely populated until many years later. The Ocklawaha swamplands were the refuge of the Seminole Indians who lived there until after the Second Seminole War when they were finally herded to the Everglades. Even after that, there were still Indian scares (Mitchell, 7). Hubbard L. Hart, a young Vermont promoter, had come to Palatka five years before and had a contract to carry mail over the stage route to Ocala and Tampa. Hart had written vigorous letters to the Post Office Department asking for military protection against ambush. The Indian talk even had Congress troubled, but it was more imagined than real (7).

Even though steamboats were flourishing on the St. Johns, none of the boats attempted to enter the Ocklawaha. The truth is the boats were not built to travel a river full of stumps, snags, sunken logs, and all manner of other hazards (7). This river required a different kind of boat from the ones that were common on the St. Johns.

A number of men had traveled the Ocklawaha on pole barges and rafts through the years, including one of the best-known Hart Line Captains, Henry A. Gray. Others were J. E. Manucy and George Allen. Manucy was later master of the *Astatula,* and Allen was Hart's first navigator.

Hubbard Hart began to look at the crooked river with interest in 1860. Among his other interests, he was a pioneer orange grower and foresaw an influx of immigrants from the North to plant orange trees as oranges were a staple item for export. He also foresaw the need for supplies of all sorts to be taken upstream to the settlers and the possibility of tourist travel to Silver Springs. With all this in mind, Hart became a steamboat man (Mitchell, 8).

The first Ocklawaha River steamboat was the *James Burt,* which Hart purchased in 1860. Not much is known about what she actually looked like because there are no pictorial records of some of the earlier boats. The boat's architecture has to be guessed at, but she probably had a skiff-mounted hull surrounded by a low, crude cabin. The boat was probably less than 60 feet in length and was a stern-wheeler. The Ocklawaha was never a side-wheel stream. Hart's second boat, the *Silver Spring,* was built in the same year for the line's inauguration. Like the *James Burt,* not much is known about the *Silver Spring,* although she was listed in the *List of Merchant Vessels of the United States of 1868* as being number 23066 and 73.91 tons. The first captain of the *Burt* and the *Silver Spring* was Hart's old friend George Allen. He was the real nucleus around which the Hart Line took shape (8).

The Hart Line started with two boats that plied their trade between Palatka and Ocklawaha and extended the travel to various parts of the St. Johns River. When United States naval forces landed in Fernandina in 1862, the business went on as usual because the St. Johns Valley was not actively engaged in the war (9). Later, the war began in earnest for the St. Johns-Ocklawaha region and its steamboats. In rapid succession, Federal forces seized the mouth of the St. Mary's and the mouth of the St. Johns for seventy-five miles above Jacksonville. The Ocklawaha was never penetrated; nor, except for occasional and usually costly gunboat sallies on the part of the Federal navy, was the upper St. Johns. The boats continued to run, but their cargos and the nature of their services changed sharply (Mitchell, 9).

James Burt became a link in the chain of communication and supplies that, after the establishment of the naval blockade, was the Confederacy's lifeline. Blockade runners were in use and the shortest route for them was from Nassau to Mosquito Inlet, Florida. From New Smyrna and other ports on the Inlet, their cargos were carried in wagons across the narrow isthmus separating salt water from the upper St. Johns. At the river landings, *James Burt* and other small steamers carried the goods down the St. Johns to Welaka and up the Ocklawaha as far as the old Seminole War post Fort Brook, which would later become Tampa, Florida. At Fort Brook another wagon train took the cargo over sheltered roads to Waldo Station on the Fernandina & Cedar Key Railroad Line. *James Burt* would be well on her way back loaded with cotton, which was the overseas currency of the South, before the wagons reached the railhead. *Silver Spring* was undoubtedly used for the same service on the supply line, but *James Burt* was not heard of after the war and there is no record of what actually happened to the boat. The fact that no mention was made of the boat and because previously she had been more actively engaged than the *Silver Spring* on the supply run was a reasonably good indication that she was no longer afloat (10–11). Hart purchased another steamboat on October 5, 1863—an additional indication that he may have lost the *James Burt*. This boat was the *General Sumter* and had belonged to the St. Mary's Steamboat Company. He paid $6,000 for the vessel and sold her three months later for $15,000 to S. G. Cabbel and four associates. The boat was to last only a few weeks in their hands. She was captured on Lake George along with all her passengers and crew by the U.S. Gunboat *Columbine*, which was on a foray in enemy territory on the upper St. Johns (Mitchell, 12).

Hart took his profit from the *General Sumter* and bought another steamboat just fifteen days later. This boat was sunk at Volusia along with all her fixtures and machinery. For all we know, Hart may have never raised her because she was never listed as a member of his active fleet. This boat was the *Emma White* and belonged to Hart's friend Henry A. Gray. *Emma White* may have been used for the lucrative blockade running that was going on at the time (12).

After the war was over and Reconstruction had begun, Hubbard Hart was a rich man and had the title of colonel by which he was usually addressed for the remainder of his life. He had only one steamboat at the time but had the means to build more. He also had the determination to continue the colonization and agricultural development of the Ocklawaha (15). Before any commercial travel could begin on the river, it had to be cleared of some of the many obstructions that had accumulated both naturally and through wartime use. The Confederates had realized its importance from a military viewpoint and had negotiated a $4,500 contract with Hart in February 1865 to remove the obstructions in the Ocklawaha from Fort Brook to the St. Johns River. The contract was dated February 21, 1865, and had March 16 as the deadline for completion of the work. This wartime work was presumably done by *Silver Spring* (Mueller, *Ocklawaha*, 6). After that, a new contract was made with the U.S. government that gave Hart federal land along the Ocklawaha in addition to money to continue the work of clearing the river. To do this work, Hart needed another boat, so in 1866 he built the *Griffin* at Palatka. Her hull number was 10835 and she was 52.2 tons. Hart's shipyard was at Hart's Point across the St. Johns River from Palatka at a sharp bend in the river. The Ocklawaha fleet would come there regularly to be repaired. There was even a small marine railway to haul vessels out of the water (6–7).

After *Griffin* was built, work began on the river in earnest. She worked most of the time with the large derrick scow *Pioneer. Silver Spring* was undoubtedly also used. The work took three years to complete and was tedious and exhausting. Commercial trips had to be made and the weather did not always cooperate. The long task was always there.

The ships and workers struggled with a river that offered a vast assortment of obstacles to navigation. They could do nothing about the hairpin curves, rapid flow, and narrow passages that sometimes went between massive cypress tree trunks. They could remove dead and waterlogged timber and masses of floating vegetation. In one fifteen-mile stretch in the vicinity of Silver Springs Run, 300 trees and 172 logs were removed from the bottom. Floating islands of water hyacinth were a big problem in the upper reaches above Silver Springs. Captain David A. Dunham, master of the *Griffin*, came up with a solution to the problem. Working chiefly in high water, Dunham towed these floating islands onto the flooded prairies and staked them out. When the water receded, the plants would take root and anchor themselves. The plan worked so well that the river was opened to navigation before the end of 1868 and remained so until the abandonment of regular service to the upper Ocklawaha (Mitchell, 16–18).

In 1869, Hart had the steamer *Pansoffkee* put in the official list and into Hart Line service. Anyone who knows the geography of Florida may wonder why an Ocklawaha boat would be named for a lake that drains into the Gulf of Mexico, in contrast to the Ocklawaha River and lake system that drains into the St. Johns and then into the Atlantic. The mystery is probably solved by a printed sheet of paper that was preserved in the old Palatka office of the Hart Line. It tells of a bill that Senator Osborne introduced in Congress on March 9, 1869, concerning the digging of a canal sixty feet wide by six feet deep from Lake Harris to Lake Panasoffkee, and the construction of locks that would pass boats not less than 30 feet in width and 100 feet in length. It also mentioned the deepening of the Withlacoochee River to make it navigable for steamboats. This could have been the first attempt at making navigation possible from the Atlantic Ocean to the Gulf of Mexico. The bill did not pass, but Hart knew about it and was ready with the steamboat *Pansoffkee* in case it did (18–19).

By the time *Pansoffkee* was ready to run, *Silver Spring* was not heard of again. Whether she was dismantled and her machinery used in another vessel or met some other fate on a lonely stretch of the river is not known, but Hart still had three other vessels and the steamboat business was beginning to boom (Mueller, *Ocklawaha,* 8).

Ocklawaha River steamboats were not pretty craft by any means. They were built to be functional and looked like a not-yet completed houseboat on a rowboat-shaped hull. They usually had two decks, with the lower one for freight and machinery and the upper one for passengers. The *Griffin's* pilot house was placed on the forward part of the cabin deck. Its most unusual feature was the recessed stern-mounted paddle wheel that was almost completely enclosed in the center of the hull and superstructure. The wheel on Oklawaha River steamboats was typically turned by a pair of steam engines, and doors opened at the rear of the vessels to let the churning water escape. Rudders were placed aft of the recessed wheel and gave the vessels good turning capability. Usually there was a single boiler and furnace to supply steam to the engines. No vessel was wider than 23.5 feet or longer than 89 feet. This was because of the narrow passages in the river they had to travel (7).

Hart's second postwar boat was the *Ocklawaha,* built in 1867 or 1868. The hull number was 19109 and she was 69.94 tons. This boat was much like the *Griffin* in that she was remodeled during her lifetime. The pilot house was moved to the top of the cabin deck for a better view of the river while the boat was under way. The *Ocklawaha* and the *Griffin* were the only two Hart vessels that had parallel rows of windows for the second-deck cabins (7).

The river was now open to travel and Hart was a richer man having acquired a lot of land for his prior efforts. He also now had his boats operating on regular schedules. A boat left Palatka every Thursday for Lake Griffin. A steamer ran twice a week from Palatka to Silver Springs. The running time from Palatka depended on receiving tourists at Palatka from the Charleston and Savannah seagoing boats. These were usually the *Dictator* or the *City Point*. In 1871, the schedule was about the same. The *Griffin* was the Silver Springs boat, leaving Palatka on Thursday and Silver Springs on Saturday for the return trip. The *Ocklawaha* was the through boat to Okahumpka, leaving Palatka on Sunday, Okahumpka on Wednesday, and Silver Springs on Thursday. She barely arrived back in Palatka in time to get ready for her next trip. *Pansoffkee* was on a new route from Palatka to Cresent Lake. It was reached from Dunn's Creek, a tributary of the St. Johns. This trip ran once a week (Mueller, *Ocklawaha*, 7).

Captain Henry A. Gray had served in the Confederate Army as a captain and on the Ocklawaha as a steamboat captain. He was one of the pioneers of travel on the river and finally wound up as master of one of Hart's steamboats. He was born in Tattnall County, Georgia, on December 18, 1826. After living there for sixteen years, he went to Savannah, Georgia, and began his career on a Savannah River steamboat. He spent two years aboard the Savannah River boat and finally bought a mule and set off for Florida. After trading his mule for a small yellow horse, he arrived in Ellaville, Florida, and found a job on the Suwannee River on a steamboat that ran from the river to Cedar Key. Henry was promoted to captain on the boat after several years. Sometime in 1849 or 1850 he had an unfortunate incident that cost him his position as captain. He ran the steamboat into a high rocky bank on the river and tore out one of the side-wheels.

Henry had every intention of going to California for the gold rush and went to Cedar Key to get a schooner to New Orleans. While waiting for the schooner, Gray met a Frenchman who interested him in a large tract of cedar timber located on Star Island in the Ocklawaha River. Star Island was thirty-seven miles below Silver Springs. The timber on it was available for purchase and offered a good financial reward if it could be brought to market.

The two men decided to investigate the timber deal and started to walk to Ocala. Walking was the only direct way to get there. Gray had $1,500 in gold and carried it around his waist in a leather money bag. He also had a small rifle to kill game for food along the way. At night they pulled moss down from the trees to use as bedding.

Sleeping on the ground gave Captain Gray a bad fever and touches of rheumatism. When he arrived in Ocala, he secured accommodations at the home of Mrs. Emma White who nursed him back to health. The illness was serious and lasted for three weeks. After he recovered, Gray and his partner bought the cedar tract and started the lumbering operation.

The cedar was cut and the logs were squared off and assembled into rafts. The rafts were floated downstream to Welatka or St. Johns and loaded on schooners to go to Savannah where they were sold. Several rafts of timber were sold and a good deal of money realized.

The partners separated after the venture, and Captain Gray went to Palatka and started a business operating a pole-barge line between Palatka and Silver Springs. Pole barging was laborious work but good profits could be made with it.

In the 1850s, Gray's family legend has it that Captain Gray operated a steamboat called the *Micanopy*. There was such a boat of 37 tons that was built in Charleston in 1853 and was documented until 1855 (Mueller, *Ocklawaha*, 3–4).

Captain Gray bought a steamboat he named *Emma White* in honor of his Ocala friend. He operated the boat between Palatka and Silver Springs hauling passengers and freight until the Civil War came to Florida.

The *Emma White* was a casualty of the war. She was sunk by the Confederates across the low water point on the St. Johns in an attempt to block the river against Federal vessels. The blockade was only partially successful. This was the same *Emma White* that Hart bought with the money he made from the sale of the *General Sumter* (5).

Hubbard Hart's steamers were not without some competition on the river in 1871. Henry Gray sold some property for $400 and borrowed the remainder of the cost to build the *Marion*. The *Marion* was more crudely made and less pretentious than any of Hart's other vessels. The official number was 90399, and she was 78 feet long by 18 feet wide with an 8-foot depth of hold and of 67.43 tons (8). The *Marion* ended up becoming a part of the Hart Line along with her master, Captain Gray, in the busy and prosperous 1880s (Mitchell, 22).

The *Marion* formally joined the Hart Line on November 8, 1880. In a bill of sale bearing that date, Henry A. Gray conveyed her to Hubbard L. Hart for $2,000. Steamboat prices had declined sadly in the seventeen years since Gray sold *Emma White*. The document describes *Marion* as having no mast, a plain head, and a square stern. She had received an entirely new superstructure and had come to resemble closely the other Hart liners of the 1880s. The sale signaled Gray's decision to step out of the independent steamboat operation and join Hart in his. He appears as captain of several Hart liners over time, including *Marion, Osceola,* and *Astatula* (30).

13. The *Marion* on the Ocklawaha River near Iola, Florida. Photo used by permission of the Florida Photographic Archives.

When the *Marion* first started her career on the river in 1875, the famous poet Sidney Lanier wrote the essay "On the Ocklawaha in May," a description of his trip aboard her to Silver Springs. Lanier was a sensitive observer and able writer whose description of the trip is noted here. "The little Ocklawaha steamboat *Marion*—a steamboat like nothing in the world so much as a Pensacola gopher with a preposterously exaggerated back—had started from Pilatka some hours before daylight, having taken on her passengers the night previous." The boat was seemingly an object of amusement for Lanier, but he writes of her with real affection as he sat with his feet propped on the rail, watching in complete laziness as unearthly landscape moved by, or listening to the night sounds of the cypress swamp. He begins again: "Our little gopher boat scrambled along side a long raft of pine-logs which had been brought in separate sections down the Ocklawaha and took off the lumbermen, to carry them back for another descent while this raft was being towed by a tug to Jacksonville." After he describes the raft men, he speaks of the vanilla-gatherer gliding out of the cypress swamp perhaps once a month to consign his personal "shipment" of hand-gathered wild vanilla to the steamboat captain. The bills drawn against the consignment are extremely primitive. He quotes one that was shown him by the captain: "Deer Sir, I send you one bag Verneller, please fetch one par of shus num 8 and ef enny over fetch twelve yards hoamspin. Yrs trly." Lanier describes the river:

> For many miles together the Ocklawaha is a river without banks, though not less clearly defined as a stream for that reason. The swift, deep current meanders between tall lines of trees, beyond these, on each side, there is water only. As we advance up the stream our wee craft even seemed to emit her steam in more leisurely whiffs, the white crane, the curlew, the limpkin, the heron, the water turkey, were scarcely disturbed in their quiet avocations as we passed, and quickly succeeded in persuading themselves after each momentary excitement of our gliding by that we were really after all no monster, but only some day-dream of a monster.

Sidney Lanier's is an apt description of a trip on the Ocklawaha on the small steamer *Marion* in the 1800s (Mitchell, 23).

Also in 1875, the *Pansoffkee* was listed as being broken up or dismantled. It seems she was too small for the regular Ocklawaha run and that is why she was used on the run to Dunn Lake instead (23). She could be spared because two new boats were ready to take her place in the line.

The first of the new boats turned out to be the Methuselah of the line and one of the longest-lived stern-wheelers of any period. This boat was the *Okahumkee,* built in Palatka in 1873. Since she was also the most remodeled and rebuilt of the Hart liners, there was a consistent misspelling of her name in the list for thirty-five years. Photographs of her prove that there was only one *Okahumkee* from 1873 to 1920. The continuity of her official number and hull dimensions plus data contained in her inspection certificates establish that fact. Even so, Florida maps and guidebooks, not to mention the correspondence of her own proprietors, officers, and acquaintances, spelled the name by which she was christened at least five different ways (26).

When she was built, her name boards bore the name *Okahumkee,* but that spelling was to change in the middle 1980s. In 1886, her name boards were altered to read *Okeehumkee,* but on the list the boat remained *Okahumkee* for the rest of her life. The vessel was named after a legendary Indian chief who was ruler of the tribes around the southwestern lakes.

Okahumkee was rebuilt in 1886 and her upper cabin structure was lengthened and widened, although it remained small. During the next seven years she received a number of minor alterations. The slat rails she originally had were replaced with rope, and middle windows on the cabin deck were installed. In 1893, the vessel was completely rebuilt. She emerged as a double-cabin boat and retained that character until her superstructure finally came down seventy years after her launching.

Launched in 1874, her running mate, *Osceola,* was also built at Palatka and, like Osceola County, Florida, named for the famed Seminole chief.

Osceola's inspection certificate of October 20, 1879, showed that her steam was generated in a locomotive tubular boiler that was 16 feet by 2 feet and 10 inches. This boiler had an authorized working pressure of 100 pounds per square inch. The stern wheel was turned by two noncondensing engines of an 8.5-inch cylinder by 2-foot, 6-inch stroke.

Okahumkee's original engine data are not available. After she was rebuilt in 1893, her certificate showed she had a locomotive boiler similar to *Osceola*'s. It was 17.8 feet by 4 feet, with a working pressure of 115 pounds per square inch and a noncondensing engine of 10.25 inches with a stroke of 2 feet, 6 inches (Mitchell, 29).

The big difference in *Okahumkee* and *Osceola* was the location of their single stacks. *Osceola*'s stack was closer to the pilot house and rather chunky like those of the earlier fleet, but *Okahumkee*'s stack was taller and set further abeam. Both boats, of course, were recessed stern-wheelers.

14. The steamboats *Osceola, Wahoo,* and *Eureka* at Silver Springs. Photo used by permission of the Florida Photographic Archives.

The original masters of these boats are not known, but in 1879 D. A. Dunham was in command of *Osceola* and in the early eighties, A. L. Rice was captain of *Okahumkee* (27).

Two other steamers may have been in Hart's inventory at some time, but there is not much evidence to support this. They were the *Tuskawilla* and the *Forester* (28–29).

Astatula became a member of the Hart Line in 1881. Like all the other Hart boats, she was built in Palatka. This boat was initially similar to *Okahumkee* and *Osceola* although smaller than either. She differed in two particular ways. In place of their double stairways to the forward deck, the boat had one steep ladder in the very center. This single ladder was blocked at the foot by a large capstan. Her cabin deck and the single cabin itself were rounded-off forward. The most distinctive difference was the cabin that was several feet narrower than the boat herself. This left a narrow full-length promenade deck that was unheard of in other Hart vessels. Later modifications replaced her awkward single stairway with a towed-out twin stairway that became standard on Hart vessels until the *Hiawatha* set a new style in the twentieth century. The same modifications enlarged her interior accommodations by expanding the cabin to her full length. Her rudimentary cabin was widened and lengthened so as to develop a second full tier of passenger cabins (Mitchell, 31–32).

Now with four good steamers in service, the Hart Line entered a decade and a half that could be called its Golden Age. For fifteen years the owners were to see new business, new routes and services, new opposition, and a new and permanent trend away from normal carrier operations. Tourists and excursionists were now the primary business (32).

The pilots were normally African Americans who were trained in guiding the steamers on the river. This Hart Line practice probably had a lot of the passengers wondering. On the western rivers, like the Mississippi, this practice would have been unheard of. Obviously the pilot's authority on an Ocklawaha boat in no way resembled the pilot's authority on a Mississippi boat. Hart's captains were always in full command of their boats whether under way or docked. Regardless of the captains and their authority, though, the man at the wheel had a very large responsibility. While policy dictated that the deckhands and the wheelman were always under the direction of the captain and that two men were always present in the pilot house, there must have been times when the full responsibility of the boat's guidance rested with a single African American pilot or wheelman. It is remarkable that members of a race who were only given the status of roustabout, waiter, and fuel passer on other rivers were so respected on the Ocklawaha (34).

One thing that must have brought enormous joy to the travelers on the Ocklawaha was the way the pilots navigated at night. Most of the travelers also had memories of the lighting of the light that guided the boat at night. It was usually an iron pot or brazier mounted on the top of the pilot house. This same type of appliance was used on the other Florida rivers until around 1915 when the searchlight was invented. At nightfall the black pilots loaded the pot with fat and pine-lighter wood and set it on fire. When the travelers saw it lit, they felt every emotion from astonishment to rapture to frenzy. The flickering light cast a Halloween-like

15. Passengers aboard the steamboat *Astatula* in Palatka, Florida. Photo used by permission of the Florida Photographic Archives.

16. The *Hiawatha* was a steamboat used by the Hart Line on the Ocklawaha River. It was built in 1904 and abandoned in 1919 at Hart's Point, East Palatka. Photo used by permission of the Florida Photographic Archives.

glow in every direction. The cypress trees and live oaks heavy with moss were eerie enough in the daytime to the first-time traveler, but at night the scene was surreal. The light was practical as well as ornamental. It made navigation possible because it cast just enough illumination for the pilot to see the river channel in most cases, or at least some landmark the captain or pilot knew (Mueller, *Ocklawaha*, 33).

Dr. S. J. Bouknight and his brother had interest in three Ocklawaha River steamboats in the 1880s. They were the *Waunita*, the *Forester*, and the *Tuskawilla*.

The *Tuskawilla* was built in Leesburg in 1875 with the hull number

145082. This boat could have been described as pretty when compared to the other Hart Line vessels. She had a polygonal pilot house, and the railings were supported on carved, turned balusters. The passenger cabin front had a large, curved, leaded glass window. Her lettering was more ornate than her competitors.' The boat ran from Jacksonville to Palatka, Silver Springs, Leesburg, and Okahumkee once a week.

Another Bouknight boat was the *Forester* which Bouknight had for only a short time. She was an 1881 vessel built in Norfolk, Virginia, and was probably a recessed stern-wheeler. The boat was registered in Jacksonville and Palatka from 1878 to 1882. She was officially listed as lost in 1882 and that may have terminated her career (Mueller, *Ocklawaha*, 10).

In 1882, Bouknight had the *Waunita* in service on a daily schedule from Palatka to Silver Springs. This boat was built in Jacksonville in early 1882 and was 77 feet long, 22 feet wide, and had a depth of hold of 3 feet. Her hull number was 80874, and she was 63 gross tons and 49.77 net tons. This boat was unique in that she had twin stacks instead of the usual one. She was initially registered at Palatka for two years and possessed a recessed stern wheel. It seems obvious she was used on the Ocklawaha River. The boat had a polygonal pilot house, double ladders from her lower cabin deck, and a single ladder to her pilot house. The vessel had a curved top front cabin deck window and her wood railings were supported by carved balusters similar to those on *Tuskawilla*. *Waunita* and *Tuskawilla* were so similar they were probably both designed and built by the same person (11–12).

Dr. Bouknight and his company were competitors of the Hart Line, but their durability and the extent of their operations are mostly unknown. Two of their boats, *Tuskawilla* and *Forester*, may have become part of the Hart Line at a later time, though there is no definitive information to support this (11).

Another Hart vessel that should be mentioned was the *Flora*. She was built in Brooklyn, New York, and enrolled in 1879 as hull number 120139. The boat was 70 feet long by 16.8 feet wide with a draft of 4.9 feet. In gross tons the boat was 86.48. She had one deck, no masts, and a plain head with a round stern. She was on local service from Jacksonville to Green Cove Springs and intermediate landings. John Clark was the agent for the *Flora* (12).

Hart along with Joseph H. Smith had acquired *Flora* by buying out a mortgage from John Richardson of St. Mary's in 1879. Smith was a born speculator and promoter of schemes and was master of one of the Hart steamers at the time (Mitchell, 41).

Because the railroads were beginning to be a factor in the steamboat business, Hart decided to expand his service. He went in partnership with Joseph H. Smith in March of 1883 to provide service from Lake Monroe to Lake Poinsett on the upper St. Johns. The partnership was called Hart & Smith's Rockledge Line. The normal heads of navigation on Lake Monroe for regular size vessels on the St. Johns were Enterprise and Sanford. The Indian River area of Brevard County was opening up to settlement, and that meant more business for the boats. The vessels had to be shallow draft in order to traverse the upper St. Johns, so *Waunita* was put in service there until Hart finished the construction of *Astatula* (Mueller, *Ocklawaha*, 13).

Waunita, though less than two years old, had been sunk in the St. Johns when Joe Smith bought her and had her raised and towed to Palatka. Upon reaching Palatka, Smith found out David Dunham was in charge of the shipyard there. Dunham had been his colleague in the clearing of the Ocklawaha sixteen years earlier. Dunham kept putting Smith off in the use of the yard and complained in correspondence with Hart that he had made a bad choice of partners in Joe Smith. The purchase of the *Waunita* seems to have annoyed everyone involved. Finally, Smith towed *Waunita* to Jacksonville with *Flora* and refitted her himself. *Flora* was sold to owners in Jacksonville (Mitchell, 42).

Astatula finally took her place on the line in January of 1885, but *Waunita* had proved her worth in the meantime carrying full loads of freight. (Joe Smith had worried she might sink or have trouble in a strong wind.)

While it lasted, the Rockledge Line was a very profitable extension of the Hart Line, but the railroads were slowly gaining ground. They had been encircling the lake region of the Ocklawaha and were pushing even more rapidly down the coastal water route from Jacksonville to the Indian River. While *Astatula* was still waiting for her boiler at Hart's Point shipyard, Joe Smith reported to Hart, "I hear they will surely have the railroad finished to Titusville by the 1st of December, but I don't think they will get the Rockledge business this winter at least" (43).

From this point on, it was a race in which the partners' object was to hold on as long as there was any profit and then to get out before the heavy losses began.

On January 17, 1886, Smith reported that the railroad was killing the business, and freight rates and passenger fares must be reduced. The business seemed to have held up fairly well until the end of the 1885–1886 winter season. In 1887 the *Astatula* was announced as a spare boat on the Ocklawaha line for the 1887 season and *Waunita* sat on the ways at Hart's Point. Hart must have realized how completely Smith was wedded to the *Waunita* and left her at his disposal. Captain Dunham insisted she be cleared from the ways to make room for other craft. Smith came up with various schemes to have *Waunita* rebuilt and put back in service, but they all failed (43).

Waunita finally ended up in Hart's reserve fleet and probably under his ownership, although Joe Smith remained her master. It is questioned how suitable she was for Ocklawaha service, but she remained there until 1899. In 1884, she had been fitted with a new wheel, and it may have been of the recessed type. The vessel was dropped from registry in 1899 (Mitchell, 44).

Although the railroads were circling the area, business was still good for Hubbard Hart, but more opposition was on the way. It came from two gentlemen who were both from prominent families in the region. They were Harrison and Howard. One member of each of these families would later become Hart Line captains. On January 15, 1886, F. F. Harrison wrote Hart a letter which he was to construe as either a business proposal or a threat:

> The people up here has been of late years having much trouble with their freight that I promised to get a boat and run it on this river, and I have machinery here stored in my warehouse to run one sixty or seventy feet long. Now if you will let me have one of your boats I will not build a boat as long as you will let me have one. I ask you this to give you a chance as I know you have plenty boats. I can run a boat as cheap as any man living. I have masters and pilot's license and can use the wheel. Now, if you will furnish me a boat and let me use it, I never will put up a line in opposition to you. Please let me hear from you. I can sell my machinery to parties on the St. Johns River, if you and I can make a trade. (Qtd. in Mitchell, 46)

Hart may have ignored the letter, but the episode is very probably tied in with another and more concrete instance of opposition that happened two years later. David Dunham, supervisor of Hart's yard, reported that a Captain Howard was building a boat that was accumulated rather than built. She was a thoroughly homemade affair; the hull was put together at Norwalk, some miles from Palatka, and the boat was launched on October

7, 1888. George Lucas did the calking of the boat, and Lucas was stolen from the Hart yard right in the middle of a job by Howard.

A week later, Howard floated the hull down to Palatka for engine installation. Dunham reports, "She is about sixty feet long and 18 feet wide on deck. She has two skegs under her transom and on her rack under her stern, and he is going to put a propeller wheel between them. It will go alright until it hits a log. All he wants to do is to get speed enough to sell her, and I think he will do that to the Harrison's." Dunham makes his final report on January 27. "He uses the boiler from the *Princess* and the *Comet*'s old engine and the *Twilight*'s old wheel. He thinks he is going to get a good speed out of her; but I think she will probably be just about the same speed as the *Astatula*" (Dunham report qtd. in Mitchell, 46).

It turned out that the boat was probably the *Alligator*, which came from Jacksonville throughout her fifteen years of service as an "Inland Passenger" steamer. The migratory circumstances of her construction are confirmed by the lists that give her building place as Palatka through 1893 and as Norwalk thereafter. She probably plied the Ocklawaha as well as the St. Johns but never did give the Hart Line any competition (Mitchell, 46–47).

One other small bit of competition was present on the Ocklawaha in 1888. It only ran on the nine-mile Silver Springs Run. A guidebook from March 1888 mentions the steamer *Elizabeth* owned by James Coons of Silver Springs. *Elizabeth* would transport any willing passenger from her home port to Grahamville for $1M—a modest rate of 6¼ cents a mile. Nothing more is known of *Elizabeth,* and she appears on no list of the period (47).

The new decade of the 1890s brought about changes in the travel pattern of the Ocklawaha that were forced on its steamboat operators by new circumstances. The railroads now reached every important spot in the Ocklawaha watershed and took what business they wanted. The Ocklawaha steamboat was no longer a real necessity to more than a few residents of the area it served. There were still some oranges to be hauled from the most inaccessible groves and a few people might find it convenient to book passage if they had business in Palatka or Ocala, but way passage on the boats was just about dead. Even Silver Springs was so easily accessible from the "back door" that it was beginning to develop a tourist trade of its own.

The one real purpose the steamboats still had was to show the travelers and vacationers the Ocklawaha itself. The river was worth seeing because it was the only accessible river of its kind in the country and was still the best way to approach Silver Springs (48). The time had arrived that the

17. The steamer *Alligator* at dock at Leesburg. Photo used by permission of the Florida Photographic Archives.

18. The *William Howard* leaving Eureka on the Ocklawaha River. Photo used by permission of the Florida Photographic Archives.

Ocklawaha must survive exclusively on "tourist trade." This meant that three changes had to be made to take advantage of the new situation: the trips had to be publicized more, the annual schedule had to be revised to reduce unprofitable operation, and the steamers themselves needed to be refurbished to make them more attractive to passengers of leisure and means (49). All of these things were accomplished over time, and the steamboaters prepared for the new era.

Hubbard Hart and his ingenious specialized steamboats received a new kind of recognition in 1892. It was scientific recognition and came from the Post Office Department, which was preparing an exhibit for the 1893 World's Fair in Chicago. They requested help in constructing a scale model of an Ocklawaha River steamboat and authorization to display it at the fair. The Post Office Department needed measurements of all parts of a ship and rough drawings. They requested information on the color of the paint, the style of the trimmings, the arrangement on top of the pilot house, and a description of the brazier for the fire that was used at night to light the way. They needed photographs of the engines and boilers and full descriptions of the stern with wheel and rudder. Hart provided all the information, and a model was built and displayed at the fair. Today the model can be seen in the ship room of the Smithsonian Institution. The model is a tribute to Hubbard Hart and all the others who followed him in the steamboat business on the Ocklawaha (Mitchell, 50).

Around 1889 the fortunes of both Hart and his steamboats were beginning to decline steadily. Financial difficulties stemming from personal problems, the loss of freight business to the railroads, the changing conditions of the trade, and a serious new competitor on the scene put Hart in a life-and-death struggle to keep the line

In 1893, Captain J. Ed Lucas became the most serious competitor to the Hart Line yet. Lucas was a proprietor on Palatka's waterfront and offered boats that could take people to the fishing grounds or to visit the big groves on the other side of the river. In 1893, he set his sights on the Ocklawaha River trade. He built a new boat that adapted the best features of the Hart boats and avoided the worst. Lucas knew the day of the single cabin was over and built his boat with two tiers of staterooms above the boiler deck. In contrast to the skimpy open deck space of the Hart liners, his upper deck had ample promenades forward, aft, and on both sides. Lucas included interior companionways to both decks for the passengers so they wouldn't be rained on, as they were in Hart's boats. The gross tonnage was twice that of Hart's flagship and the funnels were stockier and better placed. An elegant polygonal pilot house topped off the design of the new boat. The name *Metamora* was boldly lettered on the side of the upper cabin and "Lucas's New Line" on the lower. The new boat was big and handsome and was anticipated to have great appeal with travelers of the day (52).

Many thought the new Lucas boat would deal a body blow to the fortunes of the Hart Line, but the colonel was still in the fight for supremacy on the river. Long before *Metamora* was in the water, Hart had *Okahumkee* rebuilt from the main deck up. She was now a double-cabin boat and well equipped to take on any opponent. When she came from the yard, she had some advantage with respect to passenger space. Her second tier of cabins ran all the way aft from the pilot house, allowing for twelve staterooms. A new boiler permitted her awkwardly placed funnel to be moved nearly amidships. Hart also decided another double cabin boat was needed, so in 1894 *Astatula* was reconstructed. The rebuilt boat was not as pleasing to look at as *Okahumkee*, but she had the needed space for passengers that Hart wanted (Mitchell, 52).

Osceola's career came to an end after *Astatula* was rebuilt. She was apparently considered less suitable for reconstruction, and a third boat was not needed. Hart received an offer of $3,500 for her in 1893, but she never changed hands. The last year she was carried on the list was 1894 (53).

Lucas made one other attempt to bolster his fleet on the Ocklawaha with the small recessed stern-wheeler *Eureka*. She was built at Silver Springs in 1890 and was hull number 136160. The boat was 69.6 feet long and 16 feet wide with gross tonnage of 79.92 tons. Her single cabin probably had as many as six staterooms. The boat was never included in the Lucas Line's advertisements, and it is doubtful she could have maintained a forty-eight-hour round trip schedule (53–54).

The *Metamora* competed heavily against Hart, benefiting from advertising and rate cutting. Another misfortune happened in 1895 that severely affected Hart's ability to compete. The freeze that year wiped out Hart's extensive orange groves and the freight of oranges from other groves.

The cold weather caused the tide of visitors to trickle to a halt. Finally faced with the loss of his line, Hart made a deal with Lucas to consolidate the two.

Among the relics of the Hart Line is a handwritten copy of an advertisement to be published at the opening of the 1895–1896 season. It was headed "Consolidation." The advertisement announced that the *Okahumkee* and

Metamora would ply on alternate days between Palatka and Silver Springs. At the bottom appear the names of J. F. Lucas, General Manager, Lucas Line, and H. L. Hart, General Manager, Ocklawaha Navigation Company. Ocklawaha Navigation Company was the corporate name under which Hart's stock had been circulated. It was his last official act on behalf of the service he had founded and fostered for thirty-five years. And it was an act that undoubtedly saved the life of his line. It was the direct instrument of the line's survival for another quarter century when steamboats deserted the Ocklawaha forever (Mitchell, 54).

The deal was closed early in December, a few days before Colonel Hart met an untimely death as he got off a trolley car in Atlanta, Georgia. It was December 12, 1895. Earlier that year, on April 3, Captain Henry Gray, in his sixty-ninth year, passed away. His death, along with Hart's, brought an end to the pioneer era on the river (Mueller, *Ocklawaha*, 15).

The colonel's sudden death left the affairs of the Hart Line in a desperate state. It was providential that the consolidation had already taken place. Hart's successor as manager of the line had time to get things controlled and organized. His successor was R. H. Thompson of Boston, who was already a substantial partner in the ownership of the line. Thompson was Hart's brother-in-law. Hart had married his sister in 1884. Thompson was in an unenviable position because of a huge debt that had to be whittled down, and creditors had to be convinced of the solvency and sound prospects of the line. Thompson also had to learn to be the manager of a steamboat company during the busiest season of the year. He not only succeeded in salvaging the line, but so strengthened it that it was able to survive the inevitable split with George Lucas (Mitchell, 55).

When Thompson took over, the Ocklawaha run had reached a point where trade was dead or dying. However, a whole generation of visitors to the Ocklawaha wilderness must thank the Thompson family because they refused to admit defeat. They continued to operate the line for twenty-five seasons, losing money in most of them (55).

Both the Lucas and the Hart lines, the consolidators in question, were starving under the consolidation. We do not find *Metamora*'s name linked with *Astatula* and *Okahumkee* in travel literature of 1897. The consolidation was short-lived, and its dissolution was the signal of a new bitterness and antagonism between Thompson and Lucas that extended to personal animosities and left a bad flavor long after the competition had died. The competitiveness had lasted at least until 1893 when the

Metamora was sunk in a race between her and one of the Hart Line boats.

Apparently the two boats had been racing for some time before they entered the Silver Springs Run to the upper Ocklawaha. A writer, F. R. Swift, published a spirited account of the race he witnessed at the mouth of the run. He was in a small boat himself and had to make a breakneck dash down the run in fear of being crowded against the bank by the upbound steamers. He reported:

> As we rounded Hell Gate Island into the upper river the Lucas Line boat loomed ahead, with the opposition boat only twenty feet behind. It was once again the rivalry of the Mississippi boats in old Mark Twain days. The two had been nip and tuck all night long. They were now hugging each other for a spurt in the fairly open water of the last mile run. Then there would be fun. The leading boat now had the right of way and puffed along like a fat king with the asthma. The trailer could do nothing but trail, for she couldn't pass the leader without pushing her into the woods. The passengers on the decks were howling and cheering each other's hands with excitement.

The Ocklawaha was a poor place for racing and the captains, at least those in the Hart service, were noted for caution and a sense of responsibility (Mitchell, 57).

The *Metamora,* which was carrying a heavy deck load of firewood, badly trimmed and pulled around a particularly sharp bend following the north bank. Abruptly, as though struck by a hurricane, she lurched to port, her tall superstructure crashing into the overhanging trees; then, just as suddenly, she careened toward midstream and settled in twenty feet of water. Fortunately, her first stagger and the crash of breaking branches woke the captain and crew and most of the passengers, all of whom were saved except two boys, Rufus King and Walter Watson, who had been asleep in the forecastle (60).

A rescue flotilla quickly came from Welaka, three miles away, and took the shivering passengers to the wharf there. They were fed and clothed and went aboard the Hart Line *Fearless,* which had come for them from Palatka.

After it was all over, bad feelings between the two firms were again ignited, each one blaming the other for the accident. The probable cause was that the *Metamora* hit a snag, and she was already listing to port because of the firewood on the deck. Also, there was probably considerable water already in her hull that sloshed to one side when she rounded the sharp turn in the river (60).

Whether the *Metamora* was ever raised is not clear, but there is no further mention of the Lucas Line being in competition on the river with the Hart Line. The Hart Line seemed to feel the long conflict was finally over and launched their first new steamer in twenty-three years.

Hiawatha was the last of the old Ocklawaha River steamboats and was also the largest and most pretentious. She was built in Palatka in 1904 in the same style as *Okahumkee* and *Astatula* but had some features that made her seem larger and more powerful. She abandoned the square pilot house typical of the Hart Line and had a small fantail deck abaft the upper cabin and no exterior moldings along the side of her cabin at the upper deck level. There were two stacks, placed abreast on the forward part of the cabin roof where stacks belong. These features made her the most beautiful boat on the river. The others had always looked homemade because of the additions that had been made along the way. *Metamora* had once been the belle of the river but was now dethroned by *Hiawatha* (Mitchell, 61).

Hiawatha had a large passenger-carrying capability because she had ten staterooms on her salon deck and eighteen on her upper deck. The dining room was on the salon deck behind the pilot house, and there was a stairway in the after section of the salon to the upper deck.

The boiler deck was also a departure from earlier boats. In place of the single locomotive boilers of her predecessors were two water-tube boilers, each 5 feet, 4 inches long by 20 inches in diameter. These were capable of producing 170 pounds of pressure. Two engines were of the condensing type with cylinders 11 inches by 3 feet, 6 inches. Each one was capable of generating 120 horsepower. *Hiawatha* was 89 feet long and 23.5 feet wide with a draft of 4.6 feet, with 129 gross tons.

R. W. Thompson, having succeeded his brother, R. H., was now manager of the Hart Line, so the *Hiawatha* came under his care. The line now had three boats in service, having sold *Fearless* to other ownership (62).

Hiawatha's life story ended eight years after she was built, having survived many gala trips on the route from Palatka to Silver Springs. In 1912, dwindling revenues caused the Hart Line to take *Astatula* out of service and *Hiawatha* took over her duties. New competition was also on the horizon.

A new company, called the Silver Springs Company, launched a boat called the *City of Ocala*. C. (Ed) Carmichael was listed as owner and was also in control of the resort at Silver Springs. Carmichael believed the day of the overnight steamers was over. He launched the *City of Ocala* to make the round trip going from Silver Springs down the river and back instead of up the river from Palatka. It was a daylight trip that did not require the passengers to spend the night in a cramped and stuffy cabin. Instead, they would return to the springs in time to be in a good hotel during the night. Also, many visitors were now coming to the springs by car. The *City of Ocala* had an internal combustion engine and wasn't even a steamboat. The pine lighter box on top that provided light at night was now a searchlight. The boat was billed as a swift and comfortable yacht (Mitchell, 65).

The last season for the Hart Line turned out to be 1919. *Hiawatha* had punctured her bottom on a log while preparations were being made for the 1919–1920 season. The final notice came in December of that year and read as follows: "Notice, Ocklawaha Steamboat Company (Hart Line), Palatka, Florida, December 9, 1919; The scarcity of skilled shipyard help, due to the previous absorption by shipyards and industries far away, obliges this company to postpone its winter time schedule, till further notice by mail to all principal ticket agents." The notice was signed by R. W. Thompson (67). The Hart Line had lived for sixty years and its oldest steamer, *Okahumkee*, for forty-seven.

Early efforts by Hubbard Hart and David Dunham that cleared the Ocklawaha for steamboat navigation did not have severe ecological effects on the river and its ecosystem, but modern man has treated the Ocklawaha harshly. First, the forest was stripped of the big cypress trees and the headwater marshes were drained for truck farm crops. Then, sections of the river were straightened and drained, and the clear tea-colored water at the southern end was turned into a murky soup for much of the year. As agriculture increased, towns and cities grew and sent heavily polluted run-off into the river. Clean water from Silver Springs kept forty-five miles of the river a lovely and productive stream until a construction project called the Cross Florida Barge Canal came into being.

The Cross Florida Barge Canal was an ill-advised project from the start in 1964. Ecologists warned of the dangers, but greed and politics entered the picture and the project began. The U.S. Corps of Engineers constructed a dam across the Ocklawaha, eight miles from where the river joined the St. Johns. The waters backed up and spread out over the floodplain, which had been cleared by cutting down the hardwood forest and other valuable trees in the area. When the new reservoir filled, the warm shallow waters in it caused aquatic weeds to grow at great speed. Today the submerged aquatic pest, hydrilla, has filled the impoundment from top to bottom. Treatment with expensive herbicides and drawing down the water level has failed to rid the reservoir of the weeds. Since conditions on the St. Johns are closely connected with activity on the Ocklawaha, the destruction of sixteen miles of river and 9,000 acres of associated floodplain forest had a degrading effect on the St. Johns. This great river also suffers from some of the ill effects felt along the Ocklawaha (Restoring the Ocklawaha River System Ecosystem).

The barge canal was finally halted in 1971 because of environmental and economic concerns and as a result of the public's desire to protect one of Florida's great river systems. A legal challenge by the Environmental Defense Fund and Florida Defenders of the Environment stopped construction, but it took another nineteen years, a $2.5 million study by the Corps, and an outcry of citizens' voices to finally stop the Cross Florida Barge Canal. State and federal bills transformed the former canal lands into the Cross State Greenbelt for Conservation and Recreation. The greenway stretches from the Gulf of Mexico to the St. Johns River and is up to a mile wide in areas. It was Florida's first official greenway. An in-depth study by the Florida Department of Environmental Protection and the St. Johns River Water Management District concluded that restoration should proceed on the Ocklawaha River. Former Governor Lawton Chiles on June 16, 1995, directed the Department of Environmental Protection to immediately apply for permits to restore the river.

We often fail to learn from our past mistakes, but where our rivers and wild lands are concerned, I hope we take the lessons of the past and apply them freely.

Steamboats on the Apalachicola

Steamboating began on the Apalachicola River in 1827 with the arrival of the steamboat *Fanny*. Prior to that, cotton was king and was shipped down the river on flatboats. Two hundred sixty-six bales were shipped in 1822. The disadvantage of flatboats was that they could not go back upriver after they delivered their cargo, and that is the reason steamboats were so important to this river and all the others in Florida.

Captain John Jenkins left Pensacola in the *Fanny* on April 24, 1827, and managed to ascend the river to Fort Gaines by the end of July. The boat found an obstruction consisting of a dam-like mattress of fallen trees, snags, branches, and other debris but managed to cut a twenty-foot swath through the mess on its way upriver.

Fanny (originally spelled *Fannie*) was built in New York City in 1823 and was of 88 tons. She was 89 feet long by 17 feet, 4 inches wide with a hold 6 feet, 2 inches deep. The boat had one deck, no masts, a square stern, a billet head, and a round tuck. She was originally intended to be a steam schooner but was altered to become a steamboat.

Owners came and went until March of 1826 when *Fanny* migrated to Mobile, Alabama, and eventually into the hands of Captain John Jenkins. On her trip up the Apalachicola and the Chattahoochee, *Fanny* went as far as Columbus, Georgia, which was the head of navigation. She arrived there on January 28, 1828, and was the first steamboat to make the trip. On this trip or another, *Fanny* hit a sandbar a few miles south of Columbus and her boilers blew up. The sandbar was named the Fannie Bar after that (Mueller, *Perilous Journeys*, 16–17).

The second steamer on the Apalachicola and Chattahoochee was the *Steubenville*. In the summer of 1827 she made the trip to the Apalachicola and Chattahoochee rivers after traveling for four days from Mobile, Alabama, to Fort Gaines. It wasn't until February 6, 1828, that she made it to Columbus, Georgia. The *Steubenville* was 117 feet, 4 inches in length, 18 feet, 4 inches in width, and had a hold of 7 feet, 3 inches. She had one deck and a square stern and had been enrolled in Mobile in 1825. The ship could carry 700 bales of cotton or 1,100 barrels of flour and was under Captain A. J. Ward (17).

As the towns of Apalachicola and Columbus grew, it became evident that they were both destined to become the major ports of call on the river systems. A man named John Lee Williams had pointed out on a trip to Apalachicola in 1823 that "Vessels drawing twelve feet of water can enter the bay and with eight feet can approach Murder Point at the mouth of the river. This river is the largest in west Florida and the outlet of an extensive and fertile country. It will, at some future time render this bay a place of extensive business, unless the produce of the country should be directed into some other channel" (Mueller, *Perilous Journeys*, 8n.23).

According to Dorothy Dodd, who wrote an excellent history of early Apalachicola, the legislatures of Georgia and Florida passed acts to establish trading towns on the Apalachicola-Chattahoochee River system. The Georgia act resulted in establishing Columbus at the head of navigation of the Chattahoochee. The Florida act established Apalachicola at the mouth of the river. After the Indians were removed from the Flint River and settlers rushed into that region, it would become part of the trade route that had been established to Apalachicola. The removal of the Indians began on November 27, 1827, with a treaty signed at Fort Mitchell for all of the lands east of the Chattahoochee (18).

By 1829, three vessels were able to reach Columbus from Apalachicola. They were the *Fanny*, the *Robert Emmett*, and the *Virginia*. Demand for these ships was driven by the cotton crop. In 1828, 496 bales of cotton were shipped. By 1829, there were 1,200 bales to be shipped, and by 1830 the tonnage had risen to 5,000 bales. There was a marked increase every year and traffic on the rivers rose to the demand (Mueller, *Perilous Journeys*, 21).

Fanny has already been described, and it is not known if this was the original *Fanny* because she had presumably been lost in 1828.

The *Robert Emmett* was built in Louisville, Kentucky, in 1825. She was a small 61-ton steamer with a length of 79 feet, 5 inches and a width of 15 feet, 7 inches. Her hold was 5 feet, 4 inches. She had a single deck on which was a "hurricane house," a square stern, and a billet head. The trip from Apalachicola to Columbus by *Robert Emmett* took sixty hours (20). The boat had a short life and was abandoned in 1830.

The third boat to arrive in Columbus that year was the *Virginia*, steaming in from Apalachicola on May 25, 1829, after a trip of thirty-eight hours. She was described as being handsome and well built. She was 120 feet long and when loaded drew 5.5 feet of water. Her 60-horsepower engine enabled the vessel to travel 100 miles a day going upstream. *Virginia* was officially enrolled at 123 tons, 114 feet, 5 inches long, and 19 feet, 6 inches wide. Her hold was 6 feet, and she was built in Cincinnati, Ohio, in 1826. This boat also had one deck, a square stern, and a billet head with a hurricane house on the deck (21).

Columbus was growing rapidly and the population of Muscogee County was 3,507 in 1830. Apalachicola was also growing, and the steady commerce from the river was the reason.

The first steamboat to reach Columbus in 1830 was the *Baltimore*, arriving in late April. This boat was built in Pittsburgh, Pennsylvania, in 1829 and was just a year old when she ventured to Columbus. The boat was 106 feet, 5 inches by 16 feet, 7 inches and drew only 4 feet, 4 inches of water. It was thought at the time that a boat drawing 30 inches to 36 inches fully loaded could operate all year long on the rivers. This boat almost qualified. Her master was John Jenkins, and the boat was co-owned by a New Orleans resident and someone from Mobile, Alabama (Mueller, *Perilous Journeys*, 22).

Pole boats arrived frequently after September when the first load of cotton got to Columbus, and *Baltimore* again made the trip on December 17, taking five days en route, presumably to get a load of cotton for the return trip (22).

Sometime in 1830 a company of gentlemen from Columbus commissioned a new boat to be built in Pittsburgh. They were David J. Britt, Seaborn Jones, John Fountain, and five other men from the Columbus area. The new boat was named *Georgian* and was built by Peter Shouse of Shouseburg, Pennsylvania. The *Georgian* was officially enrolled as 120 tons, 114 feet, 7 inches long by 19 feet with a draft of 5 feet, 10 inches. There was a cabin on her main deck and another on her second deck. Her master was David J. Britt.

Georgian arrived at Columbus on January 12, 1831, with full freight. It took a month to travel from New York by way of the Mississippi River and New Orleans (22).

The *Baltimore* ascended the river on April 26, 1831, making the trip from Apalachicola in three days. This trip was the fastest on record at the time. Other vessels running in 1831 were the *Herald, Plaquemine,* and *Marion.* No records can be found on the *Herald*, but the other two were well known on the river.

The *Marion* or *General Marion* was an 88-ton paddle wheeler built in Cincinnati, Ohio, in 1826. The boat had a male figurehead of Francis Marion on her bow, two cabins on her single deck, and a square stern. She had been a ferry at one time and was abandoned later in 1832.

The *Plaquemine* was a small 66 tons and was built in Pittsburgh in 1828. She was 89 feet, 11.5 inches long by 18 feet, 2 inches wide and had a hold of 4 feet, 5 inches. Her original name was *Samuel Frisbee,* and she was also abandoned later in 1832 (23).

Low water conditions on the Chattahoochee caused Captain David Britt to travel to Pittsburgh in May of 1832 to superintend the building of another shallow draft boat like the *Georgian* to work on the river. The boat was 127 tons, 112 feet long by 19 feet, 6 inches wide and had a depth of hold of 5 feet. The vessel was finished in late 1832 and departed from Pittsburgh on November 24. She arrived at Apalachicola on December 28, 1832. The *Columbus* had both ladies' and gentlemen's cabins that were described as elegant and spacious. According to her survey for insurance purposes, she had 4 boilers 34 inches in diameter and 18 feet long. Her cylinder was 21 inches in diameter and the piston stroke was 5 feet. David Britt was her master and owner, and lived in Apalachicola in 1834 (Mueller, *Perilous Journeys*, 25).

About the same time the *Columbus* was being built, another vessel was announced as being on the Apalachicola to Columbus route—the *Chattahoochee.* She was a paddle wheeler of 99 tons and was 113 feet long by 17 feet, 5 inches wide with a depth of hold of 5 feet, 3 inches. This boat was built in Cincinnati in 1831 and served on the Ohio and Mississippi rivers between New Orleans and Louisville for several months before coming to the Apalachicola system. Thomas Penny was listed as owner and Joshua

Grant as master. The engine had 3 boilers, each 36 inches in diameter and 18 feet long. The engine was one of high pressure (24).

The growth of Florida and Georgia in 1833 necessitated better service for carrying the mail. The U.S. Post Office made contracts with several private parties, and steamboats were also used in the process. Robert Beveridge of Apalachicola contracted to carry the mail semiweekly between Apalachicola and Columbus. To fulfill his contract he purchased the *Versailles* and had Captain Jacob Rynear as her master to run the mail once a week. This was an interim measure because the *Andrew Jackson* was being built at Steubenville, Ohio, to take her place.

The *Versailles* was of 83 tons and had been built in Cincinnati in 1833. She was to have many mishaps during her career. When she appeared on the river, she was only eighteen months old and was described by the *Columbus Enquirer* newspaper: "She is a convenient and substantial boat, having cabins spacious and well furnished." More important, she was thought to be able to run on "26 inches of water" (26).

The *Andrew Jackson* was launched at Steubenville, Ohio, on April 17, 1833, and arrived in Columbus on June 11 with the U.S. mail aboard. She and the *Versailles* were to run in tandem with Saturday and Wednesday departures from Columbus. *Andrew Jackson* was a 98-ton paddle wheeler.

The *Van Buren* began service sometime in 1833 and arrived in Columbus in early December as the first vessel of the season carrying a cargo of dry goods. She was a 94-ton paddle wheeler (26). Not much is known of the *Van Buren*'s construction, but she was lost in a fire on December 5, 1834. She was tied up at Morton's Landing on the Chattahoochee at the time and was on her down passage to Apalachicola. One version of the event is that a runaway slave on board had set the fire and everything on board was consumed. The loss from the fire totaled $45,000. Another version indicated that the *Van Buren* was at Foster's Ferry and had some 480 bales of cotton on board as cargo. "The loss of the boat and one Negro man drowned, with another that will be hung, falls heavily on the owners. The total loss was between $15,000 and $45,000 dollars."(28) A new boat in 1834 was the *Sangamon* under Captain Harris. She was of 103 tons and was built in Portland, Kentucky, in 1832. The boat was 118 feet long by 19 feet, 5 inches wide. There was a cabin on her single deck and she had a round stern. The *Sangamon* was sold at auction in Apalachicola when she was only nineteen months old to be used on the Flint River; this river runs into the Chattahoochee near the Georgia/Florida border and connects to the cities of Bainbridge and Albany, Georgia. The boat was a shallow draft vessel that was ideal for the cotton trade on the rivers (Mueller, *Perilous Journeys*, 27).

In March of 1834, there were six steamboats making regular trips between Apalachicola and Columbus. They all had been built on the Ohio River and brought to the area via the Mississippi.

Events proved 1835 to be a significant year for Apalachicola. A seven-year rivalry was established with the town of St. Joseph to the west and north along the river. Indian conflicts began again. The rivalry with St. Joseph was because the town had a deeper harbor than Apalachicola but was not a direct route, and it was not connected to the river system used to move cotton and other products from the Gulf to the towns in Georgia. A cotton press was established in Apalachicola in January of that year that would compress the cotton into smaller bales for shipment overseas. That would keep the cotton coming until a solution could be worked out about St. Joseph.

On the river, the year began with a series of disasters that pointed out once again the need for navigational improvements on the Apalachicola, Chattahoochee, and Flint. The first one involved Captain David J. Britt, who lost his newly constructed *Eloisa* on January 6, 1835, by fire at Brown's Ferry on the Chattahoochee. The 154-ton vessel was on her first downriver trip with a cargo of 630 bales of cotton. The fire rapidly engulfed the ship, and the passengers and crew had to jump overboard to save their lives. The only casualty was the chief steward. It is not known if the ship was covered by insurance. A few days later, the *Versailles* sank while on her down trip near Fort Gadsden, Florida, a few miles north of Apalachicola.

The Flint River was not immune to disaster, either. In February the *Sangamon* struck a rock near Newton, Georgia, and sank with 173 bales of cotton aboard. Most of the cargo was saved and the engine salvaged. When the boat left Apalachicola, she had discharged her cargo at Potter's Ferry, but on her return trip, when she was nearing Newton with a full head of steam, the boat hit the rock and sank immediately. The *Apalachicola Advertiser* stated: "This is the second boat that ever ascended the Flint River above Bainbridge. Most of the rocks could be removed which would render navigation safe, but it is very dangerous in its present situation" (29).

In mid-May the *Andrew Jackson* made a round trip between Apalachicola and Columbus in only ninety-five hours, including a layover of eighteen hours in Columbus. This was believed to be the fastest trip made on the river at the time. In mid-June, seven steamboats serving Columbus delivered 12,710 barrels of cargo there and took 242 bales of cotton south.

The new boat on the river was the *Southern*. She was built in Steubenville, Ohio, and was of 133 tons. The boat was 134 feet long by 19 feet wide with a depth of hold of 6 feet. This boat could make nine miles per hour in smooth water.

In December the steamboat jinx struck again. Captain Jenkins was aboard the *Ellen* when she hit a snag and sank midway between Columbus and Apalachicola near Porter's Ferry. The *Ellen* would later be raised and would run for many more years (Mueller, *Perilous Journeys*, 32).

About this same time, the *Planter*, another new boat on the river, was also snagged. Captain John Roland managed to unload the cargo and run her up on a sandbar before she sank. The *Planter* was easily raised sometime later. The vessel was of 116 tons and was built in Pittsburgh in 1831.

The *Metamora* was another ship that went to the bottom in 1835. She snagged on her first trip while on the way to Columbus. *Metamora* was of 89 tons and was carrying a large cargo of goods on the trip. She was built in Pittsburgh in 1832 (33).

To end the year of disasters on the river, *Flossie* burned at Brown's Ferry and the *Magnolia* was abandoned in 1835 (34).

In 1836, Indian troubles plagued the area and upstream travel was hindered by the unfriendly Creeks to the north and the Seminoles to the south. Apalachicola and St. Joseph to the west were still growing and becoming more prosperous. The Second Seminole War prompted great concern in Florida, and the steamboats were to be used to transport troops and supplies around the battle areas. The army usually chartered vessels but in some cases it purchased a few. The waters of the Gulf of Mexico and the Apalachicola and Chattahoochee rivers would see their share of military-oriented steamboat activity.

Lots of land was for sale in St. Joseph in January 1836, and the steamboat *Merchant* was chartered for the purpose of showing the land to prospective buyers. People from Pensacola, Mobile, and New Orleans who were interested in buying could take the boat and see the land for themselves. The average sale price was $750 per lot, and there were over 600 lots in the original town and 600 more in the eastern section. The town became officially incorporated in February 1836. St. Joseph had great facilities for loading and unloading large oceangoing vessels, with large wharfs and seventeen feet of water in the bay. The problem was getting the cargo to the Apalachicola River after it was unloaded so it could be transported to Columbus (34). It was almost eight miles from St. Joseph to a sharp bend in the Apalachicola River known as Pinhook Bend and a place called the Depot on the north side. A canal was first proposed to connect the Apalachicola and St. Joseph, but in the end a railroad was built for that purpose (Mueller, *Perilous Journeys*, 30–31).

The Territorial Legislative Council petitioned Congress for two lighthouses in the St. Joseph area, and the town was declared a Port of Entry and Delivery after they were built (35).

On the river, another steamboat was lost on March 20. It was the *Planter*. She and the *Reindeer* came into contact on Morgan Shoals about eight miles below Fort Gaines. The *Planter* sank in ten feet of water, but only 100 barrels of freight were aboard at the time of sinking. The *Reindeer* did not sink (35).

The war for supremacy as a port continued between Apalachicola and St. Joseph as the Apalachicola Land Company planned their city and sectioned out lots. The Apalachicola *Gazette* criticized St. Joseph:

> Rumor that the Apalachicola merchants were moving to St. Joseph is without foundation. That place exists only in name and in the mind of a small band of speculators, who would build a city at public expense. If the planters and merchants on the Chattahoochee and Flint Rivers are to incur an unnecessary expense in the transportation of produce and goods on a railroad for the sake of going thirty miles further to market, and aiding a few speculators in building a town where nature has said there shall be none we have no objection, but we hope they will just take the trouble to examine the pleasures and advantages that artificial channels afford over the natural channel of the Apalachicola where steamboats and ships meet and exchange their cargos. (Mueller, *Perilous Journeys*, 35)

The years 1837 to 1839 saw continued improvement to the towns of Apalachicola and St. Joseph, and the railroad was finally finished, with the first train running in March 1839. The line extended from St. Joseph to

Depot Creek, and the creek went on to Lake Wimico. This shallow lake connected to the Apalachicola River. The state's first steam locomotive was added in 1837, but economic distress, shallow lake water, and a yellow fever epidemic combined to cause the abandonment of the railroad line in 1839. By 1840, St. Joseph was in serious decline (58–66). Even with the completion of a railroad line from St. Joseph to the town of Iola, which was some thirty miles north on the Apalachicola River, Apalachicola continued to be the port of preference and dominated the trades by a substantial margin (69). The summation of the 1839–1840 cotton season was that 30 percent of the available crop was shipped from St. Joseph and 70 percent was shipped from Apalachicola. This was simply not enough to sustain St. Joseph and was a death blow to the town (71).

By late October 1840, Indian troubles were almost at an end, but a stunning disaster happened in November with the loss of the *Leroy*. A boiler explosion caused by the collapse of a flue happened about two miles north of Blountstown. It took the lives of six people, including the captain, Washington Smith. Luckily there were few passengers aboard or the loss of life would have been much greater (Mueller, *Perilous Journeys*, 72).

The terminus of the railroad was at Iola, fifty-nine miles from the city of Apalachicola on a beautiful bluff by the river. It was described as a frontier town in the north end of present-day Gulf County on the western shore of the Apalachicola River and just to the north and east of Wewahitchka, Florida. It was originally a Seminole Indian settlement and had been occupied by the famed Chief John Blount in 1823. John Blount was a friend and guide for Andrew Jackson. Before Iola was settled, John Blount moved to the present site of Blountstown, Florida, and that town was named after him. Since Iola served as the northern terminus of the St. Joseph and Iola Railroad, a post office was established there in 1838 and it was used as a voting precinct. After 1845 the post office was discontinued and the town of Iola rapidly faded away (30).

In October 1841, the *Union* sank alongside a wharf in Apalachicola in a gale. She was later towed into the channel where she was temporarily kept and marked with a buoy.

Another sinking occurred on October 31 to the *Chamois*. Her boilers burst when she tried to get up extra steam to get across the "bar" at the junction of the Flint, Apalachicola, and Chattahoochee rivers. Three members of the crew were killed and several wounded. Captain Morton was severely injured. The *Chamois* was aground prior to the explosion and the extra steam was used to try to get her off the bar.

The *Wabash* was sunk near Ft. Gaines on her downward trip, but the cargo of 584 bales of cotton was saved and no lives were lost. The *Wabash* was built in 1841 in Louisville and was of 131 tons.

A month later the *Oriole* was on the way to Apalachicola from Mobile with Captain Woodruff aboard. He had previously lost his steamboat, the *Roanoke*, at Columbus when a tree fell across her at the municipal wharf. The *Oriole* was of 110 tons and was built in Cincinnati in 1840.

The newly built *Columbus* left Pittsburgh for Apalachicola on November 10. Captain Henry Allen was her master.

The *General Harrison* exploded in the Chattahoochee River in November and three lives were lost. Steamboating on the rivers was an extremely hazardous occupation in 1842 (31). Vessels abandoned were the *Hyperion*, *Osceola*, and *Lewis Cass*.

In 1843, ten steamboats came to Columbus sometime during the year. The boats were the *Florence*, *Lowell*, *General Sumter*, *Charleston*, *Tallahassee*, *Augusta*, *Boston*, *Siren*, *Apalachicola*, and *Robert Fulton*.

Florence was of 159 tons and built in Apalachicola in 1841. *General Sumter* was of 155 tons and built in Apalachicola in 1842. *Charleston* was built in 1843 in Elizabeth, Pennsylvania, and was of 133 tons. *Boston* was a Pittsburgh product built in 1843 and was of 137 tons.

Robert Fulton was 157 feet long and 22 feet wide with a 5 foot, 2 inch deep hold. She was of 169 tons and built in 1839 in Madison, Indiana. The boat had one deck and a plain head.

The largest load of cotton ever to arrive in Apalachicola was 1,115 bales aboard the *Augusta* in January, 1843. Captain Harris was master of the ship.

The *Agnes* was built in Pittsburgh in 1840 and was 132 feet long by 18 feet, 5 inches with a 4-foot deep hold. She had one deck, no masts, a square stern, and plain head; her cabin was above deck. This boat would float in fifteen inches of water and was well suited for conditions on the rivers. In addition, she had two engines with safety valves. She was of 85 tons.

Robert Fulton met her demise in April while coming down river. She snagged at Virginia Point and sank. The boat was carrying no cargo (Mueller, *Perilous Journeys*, 32).

The late 1840s started with an explosion and another steamboat tragedy on the river. The *Siren* was pulling away from the dock after taking on cotton and had made one or two revolutions of her wheels when the boilers exploded. The explosion tore off the complete forward cabin, the boiler deck, and the forecastle. The pilot house was lost and all that was left was a part of the hull and about half of the hurricane deck. Twelve people were killed and Captain Sharpless was blown fifty feet into the air and landed in the water. He swam ashore and was not seriously injured. The steamboat, *Notion,* came to the assistance of the survivors shortly after the explosion. The *Siren* was a complete wreck and went immediately to the bottom. The U.S. mail was saved along with some of the cotton cargo.

Another tragedy took place shortly after the *Siren* was sunk. The steamboat *Lowell* was on her downriver trip from Columbus when she struck a snag or rock and sank near Rob Roy Shoals (33).

Another year of steamboat disasters was 1845. The *Viola* was snagged and sank in the Flint River a few miles from Bainbridge. The *Viola* was of 156 tons and was built in Brownsville, Pennsylvania, in 1834. She had 1,030 bales of cotton aboard, and the cargo along with the ship was deemed a total loss. Captain H. W. Van Vechten was also half-owner of the recently lost *Siren,* so when the *Viola* went down, it was especially hard on him.

On Monday, May 3, the *Charleston* blew a boiler sixteen miles south of Columbus, but no cargo or lives were lost (34).

Vessels running on the rivers at the end of 1845 were the *Columbus, Norton, Lotus, Boston, Apalachicola, Augusta, Peytona,* and *Emily.*

The exports of cotton continued to increase in 1846. For the year ending September 30, 1845, some 153,386 bales had been exported. The total tonnage of the river steamboats was 2,400 tons.

The *Albany* was launched in Albany, Georgia, on January 17, 1846, and began making regular trips to Apalachicola. The *Flint* was launched the same year in April from the same yard. Her engines were installed in Apalachicola. Another new boat, the *Southerner,* was launched later that year and would carry 1,000 bales of cotton on four feet of water. As boats were lost, others were built to take up the trade.

The *Peytona* was the queen of the fleet that year and posted one of the fastest times. In May she left Columbus for Apalachicola and on her return trip she went from Apalachicola to Ft. Gaines in twenty-one hours and seven minutes. She made it to Eufaula in twenty-four hours and twenty minutes and on to Columbus in thirty-four hours and thirty minutes. This was the fastest time to date (Mueller, *Perilous Journeys,* 35).

The *Flint* was a tiny steamboat in comparison to some of the others. She was 83 feet long by 16 feet wide and of 31 tons. The hull was built in Albany and the engines installed in Apalachicola. The *Flint* could make only four miles per hour against the current, but she could operate in shallow water (36).

The 1840s ended with the normal number of disasters and sinking on the river system and the 1850s began with another. The *H. S. Smith* caught fire during her passage from Columbus to Apalachicola on March 24, 1840. She had a cargo of 1,015 bales of cotton, and three bales were all that was saved. Two passengers and two deckhands were drowned.

On May 22, the bark *Norma* was burned at Apalachicola while loading cotton. The fire spread so rapidly that the captain and crew barely had time to escape.

The *New Boston* was a vessel built to replace the *Boston,* which was abandoned that year. The *New Boston* was 146 tons and built at McKeesport, Pennsylvania. She was a light draft vessel that drew only 2.5 feet of water on her trial run.

The *Peytona* was abandoned this year. She was once known as the "Queen of the Rivers."

The chief reason for the port of Apalachicola was still cotton in the 1850s (37).

In early February, 1850, the steamboat *Retrieve* carried the heaviest cargo of cotton ever to travel the river from Columbus to Apalachicola. It was 1,457 bales plus fifty bales of a manufactured cotton product. There was also other cargo on board. The really amazing fact was that she made the run carrying all this cargo drawing only 5 feet, 3 inches of water.

The *Southerner* and the *Falcon* were both lost on the Apalachicola in 1850. The *Southerner* was snagged and the *Falcon* sank during a severe storm. Fortunately, no lives were lost (38).

Railroads were being built to the east and west of Columbus and on their completion would have a significant impact on the cotton leaving that city. Enough track had been completed to connect Mobile, Alabama, with the Mobile and Girard Railroad. In the spring of 1850, the Muscogee Railroad connected to the Southwestern Railroad, which connected to Savannah, Georgia. Both cities were seaports in their own right and Savannah was an Atlantic port. The merging of these railroads would transfer a great deal of trade away from the river steamboats. The railroad bridge connecting the Mobile and Girard Railroad with the Muscogee Railroad was not completed until after the Civil War. That stopped cotton from traveling by rail to the west, but on May 20, 1853, a great celebration was held in Columbus when the railroad providing a link to Savannah was completed. The first train traveled the entire route in thirteen hours, making the 300-mile trip at a speed of twenty-three miles an hour (97). As tensions grew between the North and South in 1860, steamboat trade went on much as usual. The *Oswichee* arrived in Columbus in January with 2,500 barrels of freight, and the *Munnerlyn* came in a day later loaded to the guards. After these two vessels arrived, the river fell rapidly and left both of them sitting on the bottom next to the wharf. The *Munnerlyn* was finally freed from the bottom on January 10, but the *Oswichee* couldn't be freed until the end of the month. The *Oswichee* started leaking from sitting on the bottom and one side was almost under water. She was repeatedly pumped dry and recalked until she was once again put back in service (Mueller, *Perilous Journeys*, 101).

In February, several new boats were being made ready for service on the river. One was the *John C. Calhoun,* which was launched near the end of the month. She was 165 tons and was built in Brownsville, Pennsylvania. Another was the *Jackson* being built in Elizabethtown, Pennsylvania. She was a light draft vessel capable of carrying 300 to 400 bales of cotton. Captains Hez Wingate and William Slapter were also having boats built that would be able to carry 1,500 to 2,000 bales of cotton.

Disaster again struck with the sinking of the *Oswichee* on April 14 at Francis Bend near Eufaula. She was coming downriver when the rudder post was driven through the hull as she was taking a river bend. Fortunately, there were no injuries.

Right after the *Oswichee* sinking, the *John C. Calhoun* had an explosion that killed nine people including the captain. After the explosion, the boat caught fire, drifted to the river's edge and grounded. It was a complete wreck (102).

In 1861, the coming war dominated the area, and on January 4, Florida officials learned that the Federal authorities had authorized the destruction of the United States arsenal at Chattahoochee to keep it from falling into Southern hands.

John Milton was elected governor of Florida in the fall of 1860, but assumed his post in October 1861, well after Florida seceded from the Union on January 10, 1861. Milton remained governor during the war years. A few days before Florida seceded, Governor Milton sent a group of volunteers called the "Quincy Guards" to seize the arsenal on the Apalachicola River. The raid was successful and a good supply of arms and ammunition was taken. By March 1861, there was little activity at Apalachicola. Cotton was not selling; bales worth over $1 million were stranded at Apalachicola and worth ten cents on the dollar. Two companies of volunteers were without ammunition or powder. In April, President Lincoln declared all the Southern ports blockaded.

Steamboats that were on the river were also blockaded and not able to leave the river. Confederates controlled most of the river traffic and schedules were kept. Apparently none of the steamboat personnel were conscripted into service.

Vessels serving during part or all of the war were the *Chewala, River Bride, Munnerlyn, Marianna, Jackson, Uchee, William H. Young, Indian,* and *Time* (104).

The *Chattahoochee* was one of eight vessels constructed for river defense, and others were being built not just on the Chattahoochee River but in Savannah, Charleston, Elizabeth City, and Washington, North Carolina. The *Chattahoochee* was to be completed in 120 days. The mission of the *Chattahoochee* was to penetrate the blockade at Apalachicola. That was not to be because the town was occupied by Union troops before the boat was finished. When she was finally completed, her mission changed to one of defending the river against Union forces.

A Confederate plan was devised to place heavy chains across the river at a place called "the Narrows." These chains would catch logs, trees, debris, and other material floating down the river, which would eventually obstruct the waterway. An artillery battery would also be placed at that location to keep the enemy from coming upriver (Mueller, *Perilous Journeys*, 105–108).

Affairs in Apalachicola in January of 1863 were grim. The Southerners who still lived there were nearly all women and children because all men between the ages of sixteen and sixty were now in the Confederate Army. A report filed by Federal Navy Lieutenant Commander A. F. Crossman said that the South was "most fully aware of the vital importance of Apalachicola which is now entirely unprotected. A regiment of U.S. troops could land and take possession and in a week throw up earth works which would make them almost impregnable to any force the rebels could send."

High water in December swept away most of the obstructions at the

Narrows and gave some hope the *Chattahoochee* could sweep downstream. But at that critical time, the ship's engines malfunctioned. The *Chattahoochee* was towed downstream to be used as a defensive position in her namesake town on the river. While she was being towed, the gunboat ran aground, smashed her rudder and sprang a leak. Pumps aboard kept her afloat and the tow resumed. She reached Chattahoochee after being towed twenty-four hours to go a little more than thirty miles.

For the next several weeks the *Chattahoochee* was reduced to little more than a nonpowered floating battery, and the crew performed gun drills while workmen from the Navy Yard were repairing the ship (109). A box was built that was 25 feet long and 30 feet wide by 9 feet deep to fit over the part of the ship that was damaged. A template was cut in one side of the box that followed the contour of the hull. The box was launched and weighted down to sink deep in the water. The weights were then taken out and the stern of the ship floated high and dry. A new stern post was attached and the rest of the vessel repaired (109–110).

Work was resumed on renewing the obstructions downriver from the *Chattahoochee,* and the renewed effort trapped the *Chattahoochee* forever in the upper river. On May 27, the *Chattahoochee* was ordered to make steam and go back to her namesake town after she had completed artillery practice at the Narrows. When water was pumped into the boilers, they exploded. Fourteen men were killed outright and the ship began to sink. The disaster temporarily ended the life of the *Chattahoochee.* She was a total loss, but in late 1863 she would be raised and towed to Columbus, Georgia, for repairs. After the *Chattahoochee* sank, a new ironclad was under construction in Columbus—the *Jackson.* The vessel was 120 feet long and 10 to 12 feet deep. The frame was of 12-foot-square green pine timber. Calking and laying the decks began on June 18, 1863, and the engines were ready to install by December 26. The ship would then be complete except for the guns and magazine (110–112).

As 1864 began, the *Jackson* was still not launched because of low water in the river. Various attempts to lengthen her to provide more buoyancy failed, so she stayed tied to the wharf until she was finally launched in December 1864.

The *Chattahoochee* was launched after her repairs in April but still didn't have her full complement of machinery or her seven-inch rifle. The boilers were in deplorable condition. A trip began to Eufaula, Alabama, with Captain Hez Wingate as the master. It was to take two weeks to make the eighty-five miles from Columbus because of groundings along the way (Mueller, *Perilous Journeys*, 113).

An ill-fated expedition to Apalachicola to try to run the naval blockade ended in May, and the *Chattahoochee* returned to Columbus for new boilers to be installed (115).

Most of 1865 on the river was uneventful because the Confederate cause was all but lost by January of that year. After Savannah and Fort Fisher, the war was almost over. General Sherman had begun his move on Charleston, South Carolina. The *Chattahoochee* was set on fire by her own crew when the Union forces broke through the defense lines initially established to the west of the Chattahoochee River near Girard, Alabama. They were in Columbus on the day after Easter.

After the war was over, both sides were demobilized and the Southern men returned home in much smaller numbers than when the war had begun. Some Union forces remained on garrison duty as the blockade on Apalachicola was lifted and navigational aids returned to the river. Commerce slowly returned and the vessels *Uchee, Marianna,* and *Indian* were running when river conditions would allow.

On December 31, 1866, the *C. D. Fry* made her first down trip to Apalachicola, and the *Marianna* carried heavy freight loads to Columbus. The *Uchee, Hard Times,* and *Huntsman* also made trips. The steamboat *Glide* had two engines with 17-inch cylinders and a 4-foot piston stroke. She was said to be beautiful, neat, and very comfortable for the officers and crew who lived onboard, but misfortune dogged her. She broke her shaft three miles below Chattahoochee on her up trip, and it would take a month before she was repaired.

Columbus was recovering from the devastation of the war as more and more vessels carrying cargo came to aid in rebuilding the city (121).

Another steamer destined for trade on the river was the *White Rose.* She was being rebuilt in Apalachicola after being raised. The *White Rose* was a stern-wheeler of 232 tons. She was 155 feet long by 33 feet wide with a draft of 5.3 feet. The boat had been built in Parkersburg, West Virginia, in 1862 and was called the *U.S.S. Siren* in 1864. The boat was probably the first to arrive in Albany, Georgia, after the war—with a cargo of salt, whiskey, oysters, fish, and oranges. She hoped to take cotton back on her return trip, but she struck a rock and went down with 100 passengers aboard. After she was raised, she would return to the river in May and make an appearance in Columbus (122).

In 1867, the newest boats on the river were the *Atlanta* and the *Munnerlyn.* The *Atlanta* was a 330-ton side-wheeler, and the *Munnerlyn* was a stern-wheel vessel of 193 tons.

The channel used by the steamboats at this time had shifted from the one blocked by obstructions during the war to a place called Moccasin Slough. The new channel appeared when the river diverted itself to the east about a half mile above the obstructions that were put there during the war. The slough had the appearance of a narrow, swollen creek rushing with the force of a mill race through a thick wood. Boats did not pass through until after the war when the sluice had widened enough for them to do so.

In 1867, Apalachicola was described as a town of 2,500 inhabitants with two steamers running to New Orleans and two or three to New York using the town as their shipping point. Cotton shipments in 1866 had been 114,000 bales, but the present season was lagging far behind (Mueller, *Perilous Journeys,* 123).

A disaster occurred in March when the *Munnerlyn* was sunk at the Narrows on the Chattahoochee River. There were hopes she could be raised, but she was abandoned in April.

The *Chipola* was lost in mid-September when her boilers exploded at the head of Uchee Shoals. Six crew members lost their lives and many others were wounded. By being lost on September 19, the *Chipola* had a life of just over one year.

The Merchants and Planters Line consisted of the steamers *Atlanta, Shamrock, Spray,* and *Music.* These ships served eight firms in Apalachicola, two in New York, and one in Eufaula, Alabama (124).

In 1868, the *White Rose* was no longer on the river, and in July a somewhat different vessel was being brought to the Apalachicola and Chattahoochee rivers. She was the *Julia St. Clair.* This was an iron-hull steamboat built in Philadelphia in 1866. The ship stopped off in Savannah on her trip around Florida to Apalachicola and was described as being of 174 tons with two high pressure boilers. These were 22 feet long and 38 inches in diameter—capable of 186 pounds per square inch. Her two high-pressure engines had 15-inch cylinders with a 5-foot piston stroke. She was a side-wheeler and was 129 feet long by 37 feet wide with a 4-foot-deep hold. The boat arrived in Columbus in mid-October and was owned by the Central Line of Georgia. This transportation company was primarily interested in railroads but would later own many steamboats on the river.

A running mate to the *Julia St. Clair* was her twin the *Bandy Moore.* She arrived in Columbus at about the same time. Low water conditions on the rivers kept both boats scarcely productive until later in the year.

The last year in the decade saw groupings of several steamboats into lines for more efficient operating and to open and serve new routes. In mid-March the Independent Line advertised its schedules. Boats would leave Columbus on Monday, Wednesday, and Friday at 10 a.m. for a trip to Eufaula. The return trip would leave on Monday, Wednesday, and Friday at 8 p.m. and arrive at Columbus the following day at 2 p.m. The upstream trip probably included overnight accommodations because the boats often tied up at night. The Independent Line also provided service to Apalachicola and back (126).

In early October, a new freight line started that concentrated on the railroad connection at Chattahoochee. It was called the Barnett Line and used the *Shamrock, New Jackson,* and *C. D. Fry.* One feature of this line was a connection at Apalachicola with New Orleans steamers. As the year ended, the Central Line would take the place of the Independent Line and a decade of better trade would commence (Mueller, *Perilous Journeys*, 127).

In the 1870s the U.S. Army Corps of Engineers began improvements to the rivers that would eventually help everyone who made their living on and around them. Lives were still being lost because of boiler explosions, but fewer boats were lost because of snags and other obstructions in the river.

Federal inspection of Barnett Line vessels concluded they were in good shape and perhaps even better condition than some of their competitors.

In August, the river was higher than usual and the *Bandy Moore* took advantage of the situation. She made weekly trips to Apalachicola and even had to leave some freight behind at times because there was more than she could carry.

By fall the Barnett Line's *Bandy Moore* and *Julia St. Clair* resumed trade and carried full loads most of the time, but on the night of August 31 the *Bandy Moore* struck the bank or the bottom of the river at full speed and sank. She was out of service for several weeks but was eventually raised (128). She was sent to the Navy Yard for repairs.

The Barnett Line now had the *Shamrock, New Jackson, Barnett,* and

C. D. Fry in operation making stops at Eufaula, Bainbridge, Chattahoochee, and Apalachicola.

1871 brought low water again until the end of January, when it rose so high some boats had trouble getting under some of the bridges.

Apalachicola was beginning to shake herself out of the postwar doldrums, and the boats were carrying record loads of passengers and freight when the river would allow it. Several steam-powered lumber mills were in operation and others were to begin. The supply of lumber in the region was seemingly inexhaustible, so Apalachicola was fast becoming the main supply point (129).

The government was now taking some interest in improving the navigation problems in the rivers. It began with a survey of the Chattahoochee by Captain C. F. Trill with a view to removing some obstacles in the river. This began in September with $4,800 approved for the project. A working barge was being built, probably at Columbus, to help with the work.

The surveying along the river was completed in early February 1873, and the subsequent report recommended all-season navigation as far as Columbus. The feat was not really accomplished until after World War II when several dams were built along the river. This was done long after the steamboats had ceased their operations. Indications were that the Apalachicola needed relatively little work and the Chattahoochee and Flint needed a lot. The most serious obstacle on the Apalachicola was Moccasin Slough where the Confederates had sited their blockage of the river during the war (Mueller, *Perilous Journeys*, 131).

In 1874 mail service between Eufaula and Chattahoochee was occurring twice a week and more work was done on improving navigation: $80,000 was needed for improvements to the river and $15,000 was needed to widen and straighten Moccasin Slough alone. A new $100,000 snag boat was built and manned at an operating cost of $5,000 per month (158).

The U.S. Army Corps of Engineers was active in 1875 on the rivers when the meager funds allotted by Congress allowed. They reported 108 snags and sunken logs removed from the Apalachicola River, along with some 100 overhanging trees and 1,831 cubic yards of earth. After their work on the Apalachicola, they concentrated their efforts on the Chattahoochee (135).

In 1876, river improvements were vigorously carried out. The steamboat *Clara Dunning* was working between Eufaula and Columbus dynamiting rocks from the Chattahoochee River. A raft of logs that blocked the River Styx and Moccasin Slough on the Apalachicola was also removed.

On the Chattahoochee, the Corps removed snags and overhanging trees and worked on Woolfolks Bar. They were going to construct a breakwater on the Georgia side 380 feet long, extend a jetty 235 feet, and build another 200 foot jetty to complete the work.

A yellow fever epidemic had come to Savannah, and the event diverted some business to Columbus. Columbus expected to receive 15,000 bales of cotton at the river landings—5,000 bales more than the last year (136).

The *G. Gunby Jordan* was built in Jeffersonville, Indiana, in 1877 and named after a man who was often a passenger on river steamboats. Her first arrival was on July 4, 1877. The boat was 125 feet long by 25.5 feet wide and had a depth of hold of 3.5 feet. The engine cylinders were 10 3/8 inches in diameter and had pistons with a 4-foot stroke. This boat was said to be one of the most handsome ever to grace the river, and her arrival was witnessed by hundreds of Columbus citizens. The boat would run in competition with the Central Line *Big Foot, George W. Wily,* and the *Julia St. Clair.*

The Corps of Engineers were still making improvements to the river. But their former steamboat, the *Clara Dunning,* was worn out. Her machinery was shifted to a new hull, and she was towed to Woolfolks Bar and sunk in an effort to form a breakwater which would send the water to the east side of the river so as to make the channel deeper. Despite their efforts, Woolfolks Bar would continue to be a problem. At the end of August, it was only sixteen inches deep.

For the rest of the year, the *G. Gunby Jordan, Big Foot,* and *George W. Wily* experienced good business coming and going between Columbus and Apalachicola.

During 1878 steamboating on the Chattahoochee would have a changed look. A new steamboat line emerged to lessen the control of the Central Line, and the cotton trade was substantially better (138). The name of the new line was the People's Line, and the new stockholders met on February 5 to elect directors. They met on the *G. Gunby Jordan;* they had purchased the boat for $13,400 and in seven months it had earned them a profit of $11,073. They also bought the *Big Foot* to add to the line (Mueller, *Perilous Journeys,* 139).

Not much happened for the rest of the 1870s. There was the usual rising and falling of the waters, deadly boiler explosions, and frequent sinkings.

Cotton continued to be the main cargo until the 1880s when there was an influx of general merchandise aboard the steamers. The Corps continued in improving navigation on the rivers.

In 1886, the *Bertha Lee* arrived in Columbus under charter to the Central Line. The *Bertha Lee* was a Mississippi River–type steamboat that was built in 1879 in Portsmouth, Ohio. Her master and owner was Benjamin Franklin Hall of Kissimmee River steamboat fame. In chapter 3 we described the trip the *Bertha Lee* made across the Gulf of Mexico, up the Caloosahatchee River, across Lake Okeechobee, and finally to the city of Kissimmee via the Kissimmee River. The boat wasn't very successful there and was used mostly for excursions on Lake Tohopekaliga. *Bertha Lee* was the largest boat ever to make the trip up the narrow, winding Kissimmee River.

After Hall left Kissimmee, he took the *Bertha Lee* to the Suwannee River where she was used for the Suwannee to Cedar Key to Branford run. She arrived in Columbus on February 9, 1886. The vessel was under repair in mid-March and received a new paddle wheel. While chartered by the Central Line, the vessel made three trips a week to Bainbridge along with the *Naiad*, another Central Line boat. The line had a warehouse in Bainbridge where cotton was stored until it could be carried to Savannah on the railroad at 50 cents a bale.

Bertha Lee was lost on May 2 just inside Moccasin Slough on a downriver trip to Apalachicola. She struck a log that had lodged in and was projecting from the mouth of the cut-off. The boat struck ten feet aft of the boilers and sank in ten minutes. There was little freight and no passengers aboard, but the boat was not insured. Benjamin Hall was now without a boat and broke. He returned to Kissimmee and later regained his fortunes in the steamboat business (164–166).

Steamboat activity was average in 1887. A new steamboat line called the Columbus and Gulf Navigation Company was started and two new boats built for service on the line. One was to be built immediately and the other later that summer. The usual problems of high and low water levels were prevalent.

The first new boat was the *Fannie Fern,* built in 1886, and she arrived in Apalachicola on July 13. The boat was 135 feet long by 34 feet wide with a 5 foot hold. The engines had two 13-inch cylinders and the boat had electric lights. There were twenty-eight staterooms with cabins. The accommodations were for fifty-six white cabin passengers and twenty black. The boat had a freight capacity for around 800 bales of cotton (167–169).

Better trade conditions on the rivers arrived in 1889; this was also the year that saw the dissolution of the "pool" concept—when steamboats were loaned between the different lines when they were needed. The disappearance of these lending agreements, which were formed in 1887, caused a river war to erupt in October. The cause was believed to be the refusal of the Central Line to haul freight to Bainbridge (where a rival railroad ran). This refusal took a sailing day away from the People's Line (Mueller, *Perilous Journeys*, 173).

During the 1890s, the steamboats moved from carrying cotton as their major product to carrying a lot more general merchandise. There were fewer and fewer bales to be hauled because the railroads were now the principal mover of cotton. However, there were excursion trips to be taken on the rivers, and there was still cargo to be moved, such as oysters, lumber, and ice from new ice plants constructed in Columbus and Apalachicola. The lumber industry in Apalachicola turned out large quantities of wood shingles that were moved on the boats. Just about everything in the category of general merchandise was carried by steamboat.

In 1893, the Corps continued to improve the rivers and completed a record number of projects. On the Apalachicola, fifty-two snags and 708 overhanging trees were removed. On the Chattahoochee, thirteen snags, seventy-five trees, and fifty-two stumps were removed. Most of the effort centered on the Chipola Cutoff. Here hundreds of snags and 2,832 overhanging trees, 61 stumps, and 403 bushes were removed. In Lee Slough (which was the lower three miles of the Chipola River), 3,028 snags and 1,218 stumps were taken out along with 4,452 overhanging trees and 2,528 bushes. On the Flint River 255 overhanging trees and 89 snags were taken out; 2,440 cubic yards of rock were excavated.

Just below Columbus on the Chattahoochee, 409 snags were removed and 1,113 overhanging trees. Many yards of rock and dirt were removed, and the Corps engineers stabilized the banks by planting trees and reinforcing the shore with rocks. A grand total of $100,000 was spent on navigation improvement along the rivers (174–179).

The year 1894 was one of "dullness" along the rivers. Most of the old boats were still operating and there were few casualties or disasters.

The Corps of Engineers acquired a new snag boat named the *Flint*. She was 94 feet by 24 feet with a 4-foot draft and was built at Burdock's landing about twelve miles south of Columbus. This boat was a stern-wheeler and was of 102 tons (182).

The year 1895 was good and prosperous on the rivers. There was a new vessel, the *J. F. C. Griggs,* being built in Apalachicola and again there were no major disasters. The *J. F. C. Griggs* was launched on September 8 and was named after James Fenimore Cooper Griggs, a merchant of Apalachicola and mayor.

Continuous low water in the rivers forced freight rates on cotton to be increased to 75 cents a bale, flour to 15 cents, and other freights in proportion. This would last only during the low water season when the steamers could not bring full loads to Columbus (183).

Two new vessels came to the rivers in 1896: the *City of Columbus* and the *R. L. Hill.* There was also another steamboat line called the Queen and Crescent Navigation Company.

The *City of Columbus* would run the river between Apalachicola and Chattahoochee. She started life as the *Charles D. Shaw* and was built in Jeffersonville for the Natchez and Bayou Sara trade. She had spent her last years doing odd jobs and carrying sightseers in the excursion business around Natchez after she was remodeled and became the *City of Columbus.* The boat was 186 gross tons, and was 132 feet long by 25 feet wide with a draft of 4.3 feet.

The *R. L. Hill* was a new, smaller vessel used for short local trips from Columbus to Florence, Alabama, and Hatcher's Landing on the river. She was built in Carrabelle, Florida, and was a side-wheeler of 52 tons. The boat was built in 1896 and was 90.5 feet long by 26 feet wide with a 3.8 foot draft (Mueller, *Perilous Journeys,* 184–185).

In 1897, two steamboats met their demise within two days. They were the *City of Columbus* and the *J. F. C. Griggs.* They sank at the end of March and the first of April. The *City of Columbus* was lost around midnight on Tuesday, March 30, about two miles above Gordon, Alabama. Although no lives were lost, she was deemed a total loss. The boat was on the up trip from Apalachicola and was carrying U.S. mail and a small amount of freight.

Two days later, the Independent Line lost the *J. F. C. Griggs.* Three crew members lost their lives. The boat struck a log embedded in the stream. The collision drove the log through the hull and the upper deck (186).

The year 1897 was dismal, but 1898 brought increased trade prospects when the year started with higher water in the rivers. New steamboats were built, including the shallow draft vessels *Bessie Clary* and *Thetis*. The *J. W. Hires, Three States,* and *W. C. Bradley* were added as moderate draft vessels.

The year 1899 also began with a lot of optimism and a record number of steamboats on the rivers. A disastrous fire would destroy some of them on March 22. The *Bay City, C. D. Owens,* and *Flint* were at a Columbus wharf when the fire started early in the morning. The *Flint* was the first boat to catch, then the fire spread to the *C. D. Owens* and *Bay City*. All three boats were set loose and allowed to drift downstream, and all were reduced to ashes (193–194).

At the beginning of the 1900s, steamboating on the rivers would start to decline, but it lasted for twenty more years before other forms of transportation such as the automobile and truck finally took over. This decrease in trade and traffic for the steamers was happening on all the Florida rivers at about the same time.

The first year of the decade saw activities much the same as other years. There would be continuing struggles between the independent owners and the owners who were using the "pool" system. Ownership changes and shifts in cargos would continue as time went on. The rest of the 1910s was basically the same as the first year (Mueller, *Perilous Journeys*, 197–229).

When the 1920s arrived, it was really the twilight for steamboats on the rivers. In 1922, there were 238 trips made by steamboats and small launches on the Apalachicola. There was one steamboat on the Upper Chipola River in 1922, and she made around fifty-two trips.

Two steamers still ran on the Flint River and made 196 trips. Rafts had returned to the rivers, with 287 of them making downstream trips to Apalachicola.

The old steamboat, *Tarpon,* completed her 1,000th voyage having traveled a record 700,000 miles. She made her first trip on December 13, 1902, and continued with one round trip per week for fifty weeks, making fifteen stops along the way. This boat was an oil burner that had ten staterooms and was capable of carrying thirty passengers (249).

In 1924, the Apalachicola Bay area saw more small vessels as the lumber business declined. Four sailing vessels used the port for cargos. There were 371 trips made by fishing boats and 2,700 trips by motor boats. Three steamboats plied the Apalachicola and made 248 passages.

19. The *W. C. Bradley* was a boat typical of those on the Apalachicola River. Photo used by permission of the Florida Photographic Archives.

At the end of the 1930s, the *Barbara Hunt* came to the river system, but she did not last long. She sank sometime in 1940 just south of U.S. 90 (Victory Bridge at Chattahoochee). Some of her remains are still there. The *Barbara Hunt* was of 223 tons and was 138 feet long by 32 feet wide. She had a depth of hold of 4.9 feet. The boat was a steel-hull stern-wheeler. She was one of the last steamboats to operate on the Apalachicola, Flint, and Chattahoochee River system (251).

A very detailed account of steamboats on the Apalachicola, Flint, and Chattahoochee rivers can be found in a book by Edward A. Mueller titled *Perilous Journeys: A History of Steamboating on the Chattahoochee,*

Apalachicola, and Flint Rivers, 1828–1928. This fine book is now out of print but can still be found at rare book dealers. The information I have related here is based on *Perilous Journeys*, but I only recorded the highlights of the period as I saw it.

7

Steamboats on the Indian River, Suwannee River, and Other Places

The Indian River is not really a river, but rather a lagoon that stretches more than 140 miles from Mosquito Inlet in the north to Jupiter in the south. It has three natural inlets from the sea. Steamboats operated there until well after the railroads came to the region.

Even though the region is protected by a long barrier island on the east and swamps and wetlands of the St. Johns River to the west, it remained largely unsettled for many years. Only a few hardy pioneers ventured into the region traveling its length by any means of transportation they could devise. They came aboard flatboats, sailboats, and small skiffs carrying their meager belongings, or inland by foot, oxcart, or wagon. The rest of the nation was undergoing a technological revolution, much of which would not reach this region until the 1920s.

Steamboat whistles began to be heard along the river in 1877 with the arrival of the *Pioneer*. This boat kicked off the revolution in transportation along the Indian River. For the next fifty years more than 200 different boats would follow in her path.

The golden age of steamboats was from 1880 to 1899, when over twenty-five steamboat companies would set up business and bring dozens of steamers to the lagoon. There were no paved roads in those days, and the railroads were creeping southward only slowly. Carrying large cargos and passengers rested solely on the steamboats.

When the steamboats arrived, almost every small settlement on the river extended their docks into the middle of the river to make it easier to catch the attention of boat captains and to signal them to stop. All these towns had one thing in common: they all looked to the steamboats for contact with the world beyond their doorsteps (Hopwood, 2–3).

Any time a steamboat made a trip up or down the Indian River, it made numerous stops along the way. Some landings were merely cleared places along the bank, but some had docks that extended hundreds of feet into the lagoon. There were more than one hundred landings along the river that marked large and small settlements. Every family along the river had some sort of a landing for their own boat or for the steamboats.

The longest dock was the Melbourne Municipal Pier. It stretched for 1,500 feet into the river. Over time it was smashed and suffered extensive damage when it was rammed by the boats. The pier was built in 1889 and was promptly hit by the steamer *Georgiana* in the spring of 1890. The pier is the only one remaining after the steamboat era and was restored in 1984.

The families, merchants, and cities were proud of their docks and maintained them meticulously. A sign was usually placed at the end, and early communities added the word "landing" to the town's name to ensure that there would be visitors by steamboat. In north Brevard County there were Carlile's Landing and Pace's landing. Merritt Island had Lotus Landing and Footman's landing (9).

The *Pioneer* was a small steamer of only 44 tons and was brought to the Indian River sometime in 1876. Her life was short because she burned one evening in 1877. Why Captain Thomas J. Lund brought her there to begin was originally a mystery, because only 250 people lived between Eau Gallie and Key West in the late 1870s. Most of them lived along the Indian River and had their own sailboats. Even the women and children learned to sail these boats, and they were used for transporting what little cargo was needed by the settlers.

The *Pioneer* was used during the Civil War for making runs up and down the St. Johns River from Jacksonville to Enterprise. When she was purchased by Captain Lund and his Lund-Pioneer Steamboat Company, she ran from Jacksonville to a place called Salt Landing that was about eight miles above Titusville.

Captain Lund also operated the steamers *Volusia, Daylight,* and *Fox* on the St. Johns during the post–Civil War period. He apparently made a good business decision by bringing the *Pioneer* to the Indian River. He had a vision as to what the region was later to become (Hopwood, 3).

Many historians credit Henry Titus, whom Titusville was named after, with opening the first hotel along the Indian River. That distinction belongs, however, to T. J. Lund. He opened the Lund House Hotel on Main Street in Titusville, and it lasted to serve his steamboat passengers until 1895 when it burned in a fire. The Titus establishment was a boarding house, whereas the Lund House provided sleeping rooms, a restaurant, and a saloon. A sign posted inside the Lund House noted that a bath, a bottle of whiskey, or a sack of oranges could be purchased for fifty cents. The Lund House was to be used by the passengers on Lund's steamboat and others for many years (5).

When Lund decided to take the *Pioneer* through the shallow Haulover Canal to link the southernmost point of the St. Johns River with the Indian River, it was a major decision that opened the way to future commerce along the river. This canal was located on the narrowest part of Merritt Island. It linked the Mosquito Lagoon on the east with the Indian River on the west. The federal government constructed the canal in 1854 for $5,000 to serve as a crossover point for travel down the inland waterway. Before its construction, cargo was carried across the island and then loaded on boats to be moved southward. The original canal, constructed by a local citrus grower and his slaves, was only three feet deep, and ten- to fourteen-feet wide. A new Haulover Canal was built in 1884 nearly a mile to the north, but the old canal was used for thirty years and served as an important link in Florida's inland waterway system (Historic North Brevard Florida).

Shortly after the *Pioneer* began service on the river, she struck a submerged object and was laid up for repairs. Passengers anxiously awaited resumption of her regular trips between Titusville and Sebastian, then called New Haven. The twice-weekly trips demonstrated the possibilities of increased transportation in the region.

On April 19, 1877, the *Daily Times Union* newspaper reported that the steamer had caught fire and burned to the waterline. Despite his loss, Captain Lund continued to operate steamboats on the Indian River. By the time the railroad came in 1885, he owned several parcels of land in downtown Titusville and had entered politics. He served terms as alderman and mayor of the city, and on May 8, 1898, when he died, he was in the middle of a term as mayor. His enterprises were so significant in reshaping the face of the Indian River region that they could be compared to Henry Flagler's railroads in the development of the area (Hopwood, 5).

Following Lund's lead, other steamers began operation on the river. One of the earliest after the *Pioneer* was the *Border City*. Not much is known about this boat except that she arrived with her first load of passengers on November 5, 1877, after making the run from Jacksonville to New Smyrna. The vessel had accommodations for thirty-six passengers, and the fare from Jacksonville to New Smyrna was $6. The *Border City* also made two or three trips to Titusville each year (10).

A more luxurious steamboat was the *Cinderella* that arrived in Titusville on September 17, 1882. She was a fast, light draft, steel-hull steamer that was 115 feet long and propelled by two 45-horsepower engines that gave her a speed of ten knots over the water. The boat had a 25-foot beam and a draft of 32 inches. She was built in Bordertown, New Jersey. The *Cinderella* had ten staterooms, a large food pantry, and a saloon. The upper deck was furnished with seats all around, and a raised awning completely covered it.

Even though the *Cinderella* seemed perfect for the Indian River trade, she had problems negotiating the shallow parts of the river simply because she was too heavy. She could not squeeze through the Haulover Canal in the northern reaches of the river. After a year on the river, Captain W. A. L. Ostrander took her to the deeper St. Johns River to begin service there. *Cinderella* left the Indian River for good on November 20, 1883 (10).

After the *Cinderella* left for the St. Johns, two more steamboats came on the scene. They were the *Indian River* and the *Haulover*. These boats were much more suited for the shallow waters because of their 12-foot beam and 60-foot length. At first, the *Haulover* would haul freight and passengers down the Halifax River and through the Mosquito Inlet to the Haulover Canal. The *Indian River* would then take the passengers and freight on to Titusville and all points south. As noted before, the United States government dredged a wider and deeper Haulover Canal in 1884, so both boats could be used for the entire run.

The *Haulover* and *Indian River* were both owned by the Fischer family of Titusville who operated the boats for around five years. When the Jacksonville, Tampa, and Key West Railroad came to Titusville, the boats served as the railroad's southernmost link. This railroad was to acquire the Indian River Steamboat Company. When that happened in June of 1889, it put an end to operation of the *Indian River* and the *Haulover*. The new company had greater resources and more boats, and it soon became the dominant steamboat operation on the river (Hopwood, 11–12).

The Jupiter and Lake Worth Railroad joined the Jacksonville, Tampa, and Key West Railroad to become what was known as the Tropical Trunk Line. The line started in Jacksonville, where passengers and freight took the J. T. and K. W. Railroad to Enterprise. It branched off the main line in Enterprise, so passengers were required to disembark and board the Indian River Express for the forty-mile trip to Titusville. If they wished to travel farther south, the passengers would get off at Titusville and board one of the steamboats the company owned. Five steamboats were available at Titusville depending on the day and the hour; passengers might board the *Rockledge*, the *Georgiana*, the *St. Lucie*, the *St. Augustine*, or the *St. Sebastian* for the 140-mile journey to Jupiter (12).

In those days, Jupiter was a small village that had a lighthouse, a hospital, and a few houses. There was no place for overnight stays except for the steamboat *Chattahoochee* that was anchored there as a floating hotel. The *Chattahoochee* was owned by the Indian River Steamboat Company (13).

Jupiter was also the northern headquarters for an 8.5-mile railroad line called the Celestial Railroad because of its four stations that were named Jupiter, Venus, Mars, and Juno. The railroad was, in reality, the Jupiter and Lake Worth Railroad since it started in Jupiter and ended at Lake Worth. The Indian River Steamboat Company also owned this operation. The Venus and Mars stations were nothing but sidings with loading platforms. Juno, at the northern tip of Lake Worth, served as a connection to the Lake Worth Transportation Company that served the small towns to the south with its steamboats and a sailboat a traveler could take to Lantana. There the people could take the stagecoach twice a week to Fort Lauderdale. The whole operation was called the Tropical Trunk Line system and served Florida's east coast until Henry Flagler built his railroad along that coast in the 1890s. The Tropical Trunk Line, with all its multiple connections and sometimes discomforts, was a major step forward for travel along the Indian River (13).

Richard P. Paddison came to Titusville from North Carolina with his family in 1886. Paddison would figure prominently in the development of travel on the Indian River in the years to come. He was forty-seven years old when he came to Florida. Paddison was captain of the steamer *Rock-*

ledge, which he owned and brought to Florida to link up with the Jacksonville, Tampa, and Key West Railroad as the flagship of the Indian River Steamboat Line (Indian River Historical Cruise).

Richard Paddison was a stockholder in the Tropical Trunk Line and superintendent of the Indian River Steamboat Company in December 1885.

The *Rockledge* was built on the Cape Fear River between Wilmington and Fayetteville, North Carolina. She was 136 feet long with an iron hull. The boat was a side-wheel steamer with independent engines. When she was bought to begin service on the Indian River, the boat was named the *Governor Worth* and was serving on the Jacksonville to Sanford run on the St. Johns River. After being completely refurbished the vessel was named the *Rockledge.* The work included new guards, upper works, and repainting. The *Rockledge* arrived on July 28, 1886 (Hopwood, 13).

The *Rockledge* soon became known as the "Queen of the River" because she was a favorite among the residents there. She brought freight and mail to Melbourne six days a week, and the arrival of the *Rockledge* was looked on as a great event in the daily lives of the people.

In February 1888, President Grover Cleveland visited the Indian River area, and the steamer was used to transport him and his party on a tour of the area. The vessel was decked out with flowers and bunting in the salon and dining room. Mrs. Cleveland commented, "It surpasses anything we have seen in the state." There was an exhibit of moss, flowers, and fruits from the Indian River area that was commented on by the entire presidential party.

After the president and his party settled in, the *Rockledge* made her way southward on a perfect Florida day for steamboating and arrived at the dock of Gardner S. Hardee. Mr. Hardee and his family had set up tables under the live oak trees in his yard and at 11:30 a.m. gave the president and his wife a taste of real Southern hospitality with food and drink fit for a king. A more formal reception and luncheon was held later at the Hotel Indian River at the conclusion of their tour.

After the affair with President Cleveland, the *Rockledge* was sold to Captain E. E. Vaill of City Point and became a freighter. The once-proud "Queen of the River" was no longer carrying passengers and delighting everyone who saw her on the river. Now, she labored under a burden of commercial cargo.

Sometime in 1889 Captain Vaill was informed by his chief engineer that the boat needed a new boiler and a complete overhaul. Vaill didn't want to invest the money, so the *Rockledge* was towed to the extreme end of the Indian River and turned into a floating hotel. The vessel was renamed the Lake Worth Hotel, and her career as a steamboat was over.

When Henry Flagler brought his railroad to Lake Worth and Palm Beach, the *Rockledge* was towed to Fort Pierce and later to Stuart to be used by the railroad as housing for its workers. When Flagler decided to move farther south, the *Rockledge* was towed to Miami and served as the new city's first hotel. She was used for years as a hotel until land-based hotels were built. Finally, in 1913, the boat was towed out to sea and sunk (Hopwood, 15).

After the *Rockledge* was sold to Captain Vaill, the *S. V. White* was purchased by the Indian River Steamboat Company and put on the entire river route. The *S. V. White* was named after a wealthy Wall Street financier. She was a small boat only 75 feet long and 18 feet wide, but she had a draft of only 30 inches, making her able to steam through the Indian River narrows at full speed. Her master was Captain Charles Fischer, the son of Captain Herman Fischer who was a famous river man. Later the *S. V. White* would serve as a mail boat and a tow boat, and she continued to work the lagoon after the Indian River Steamboat Company was out of business (16–17).

Sometime in 1889 a new queen began her reign on the river under the Indian River Steamboat Company banner. She was the *St. Lucie*. The vessel was built in Wilmington, Delaware, for a cost of $30,000, and sailed under the command of Captain Steve A. Bravo. She had fourteen staterooms and a large hurricane deck, and she could travel 10.5 knots over the water. The vessel drew only 35 inches of water and was able to travel almost anywhere in the Indian River Lagoon. *St. Lucie* was 122 feet long and had a beam of 24 feet.

On January 12, 1889, the *Jacksonville Times-Union* gave a glowing and detailed description of the *St. Lucie*:

> She is built on the same plan of many Ohio River steamers, having three decks. She is a stern wheel vessel propelled by two high pressure engines situated aft on the main deck. The forward part of this deck is occupied by the boiler and freight is stowed between.
>
> By a flight of stairs the saloon is reached; the cabin extending almost the whole length of the boat. The forward and after parts of the cabin are pleasant sitting rooms, comfortably fitted with easy chairs

> and settees of rattan, and antique oak card tables. On either side of the central portion of the saloons are the staterooms, the space between being used as a dining hall and promenade. The wood work of this saloon is painted white trimmed with gilt. The staterooms are 6 x 6 and very comfortably fitted up. Each contains two berths, with woven wire springs and soft, comfortable mattresses and pillows. The ceilings of the decks are lined with life-preservers. For the daylight hours passengers could take advantage of the hurricane deck which is more spacious than is customary for steamers for northern waters, and offers a pleasant promenade. Here are located deck chairs and tables to make the passengers comfortable and in addition, bright colored awnings are hung around this deck, which offer protection from rain and other elements. (Hopwood, 16–17)

The *St. Lucie* was such a success that she was quickly joined by two new sister ships: the *St. Augustine* and the *St. Sebastian*. All of the boats on

20. Steamboats on the Indian River were named after the cities they served. Here are the *St. Sebastian* and *St. Augustine* at anchor in the Jupiter area. Photo used by permission of the Florida Photographic Archives.

the Indian River Steamboat Company line were named after Indian River towns.

The *St. Augustine* was a steel-hull vessel of 110 feet length with a 24-foot beam, and she turned out to be one of the fastest on the river. Even though there were no steamboat races on the river, the crews kept meticulous records of how fast each steamer negotiated the routes. The *St. Augustine* continuously bettered her records. Although she wasn't the handsomest steamer, she was the speediest.

The *St. Sebastian* was 20 feet longer than the *St. Augustine* and a favorite of the *Jacksonville Times Union* newspaper. The *Times Union* dubbed her the "handsomest steamboat ever seen in Florida waters" although she was slower than some of the others. An attempt to increase her speed began by removing some of the inside woodwork and strengthening the paddle wheels. The lighter weight did make the boat a bit faster (18).

The Indian River Steamboat Company lasted until 1895 operating its three steamers on the river. The three boats suffered different fates as the company was declared insolvent and the assets sold to satisfy the creditors.

A new steamboat company called the Indian River and Biscayne Bay Navigation Company was formed by a group of Boston bankers. They owned the *Progress* and purchased a freighter named the *Sweeney*. The *Sweeney* was renamed the *Della*, and she was used mostly for freight. The *Progress* could carry both freight and passengers. When the new company was formed, the golden era of steamboating on the Indian River was almost over.

In 1898, the *St. Sebastian* was put back in service on the river for a short time. She later would be switched to the Atlantic Ocean for runs to Key West. Instead of passengers, the *St. Sebastian* would carry soldiers, mortar shells, and artillery rounds to be used by the American Army in the Spanish-American War. The *St. Sebastian* ended her days as a ferry in Fernandina, Florida.

The *St. Augustine* had been bought by the Indian River and Biscayne Bay Navigation Company and used for passengers until operating her was no longer profitable. She rusted away until she was only a pile of junk at a pier on the Loxahatchee River (19).

The *St. Lucie* was lost in 1906 in a hurricane. There were some survivors, but the actual number of dead will never be known because no passenger manifest was kept (Hopwood, 21–22).

After all the great Indian River passenger-carrying steamboats were gone, steam-powered freighters became the norm, though they sometimes carried passengers along with freight.

The *Santa Lucia* was one of the best-known freighters of the late nineteenth century. She was 200 feet long by 30 feet wide and had three decks and two smokestacks. Captain R. P. Paddison purchased the steamer from a company in Pittsburgh, Pennsylvania, when he was superintendent of the Indian River Steamboat Company. He completed a 2,200 mile voyage when he brought the boat from the Ohio River through the Gulf of Mexico and finally to Fort Pierce, Florida. When the boat got to Biscayne Bay, she demolished a dock and inflicted heavy damage on a small boat in the harbor, the *Roslyn,* because of her large size and inability to turn in a short distance.

The *Santa Lucia* was purchased by the Florida East Coast Railroad when Flagler's railroad came to that part of Florida. Flagler used the boat to transport railroad supplies and building materials from Eau Gallie to Lake Worth to build two hotels at Palm Beach. In 1895, the *Santa Lucia* and another freighter, the *Sweeney,* were transferred from the Indian River to Lake Worth for transporting building materials to the new town of West Palm Beach.

The *Santa Lucia* was sold to a company on Florida's west coast after her job on Lake Worth and was often seen on the route from Tampa to the Caloosahatchee River. In 1903, the boat was sold to the United States Medical Corps for use as a quarantine ship during a violent yellow fever outbreak and finally sank in Key West Harbor in 1909.

The *Sweeney* was built in Abbeville, Georgia, in 1888, and used by her first owner to haul cotton (22). She came to the Indian River on October 28, 1890, to carry passengers and freight.

The *Sweeney* was 134 feet long with a 34-foot beam and a draft of only 22 inches. She could run a steady twelve knots and had a commodious salon, beautiful staterooms, large decks with awnings, and a large dance floor for the passengers.

Her first run almost ended in disaster. It was on November 18, 1890, with thirty passengers aboard that she left the wharf in Titusville on her way to Rockledge. On the return trip she encountered stiff north winds. When she attempted to reach the dock, she went aground at the east end. The boat stayed there all evening, but in the morning Captain Paddison rocked the boat back and forth until she came free of the mud.

When the freight was delivered in Titusville, Paddison started home to New Smyrna. While maneuvering in the shoals between the wharf and the channel, a hidden obstacle severed one of the chains to the boat's rudder and the crew made emergency repairs. It took three hours before the steamer could continue to New Smyrna. The next morning Paddison encountered another problem. There was not enough wood for the return trip to Titusville. After a long delay he was finally able to get under way.

Because the Indian River Steamboat Company was owned by the Jacksonville, Tampa, and Key West Railroad, the railroad would only accept freight that had been carried by its own steamers. As a result, the *Sweeney* was forced to have New Smyrna as her home port to make connections with the Orange City and Atlantic Railroad. Other steamers operating in the area had the same problem.

The *Sweeney* had a sister ship named the *Denny*, but the *Denny* was the less desirable vessel because of her 36-inch draft which increased her likelihood of going aground in the lagoon on a run (Hopwood, 23).

As the Indian River area developed, the growing population increased the need for freighters. The Indian River Steamboat Company brought in a 140-foot steamer with a beam of 30 feet. She was the *Progress,* under the command of Captain Steve Bravo. This boat was designed as a freighter and registered at 700 tons capacity. Crews assigned to the *Progress* were considered to be less skilled than the crewmen of the passenger boats. Their pay was less and the crew members frequently came and went.

The operation of the *Progress* was profitable for the Indian River Steamboat Company until they went broke in 1896. The steamer was tied up and later stripped of her engine, equipment, and accessories in Eau Gallie harbor. In 1902, she caught fire and burned to the waterline (24).

The "Ugly Duckling" of the Indian River was the *Loxahatchee.* She was also the largest and most unusual boat ever to ply the waters of the area. The *Loxahatchee* was built by the Jacksonville, Tampa, and Key West Railroad to transport railroad equipment from Titusville to Jupiter. She was also used as a barge to service the other boats owned by the railroad. The *Loxahatchee* was built in Titusville from machinery that was taken from the steamboat *Picolata.* She had a crane and pile driver aboard that were used to build piers and docks along the river.

In addition to the huge load of freight the *Loxahatchee* could carry, her long square bow allowed the boat to land freight on shore in as little as two feet of water.

The name *Loxahatchee* might come from a combination of the Spanish and Seminole Indian words *loco* and *hatchee*. Together they could mean "Crazy River." In reality, the words mean nothing and came from the carpenter who painted the name on the bow of the boat after she was built (26–27). The carpenter dreamed up the name himself.

Other steamboats came and went on the Indian River system, but the railroads brought it all to an end during the twentieth century, as on all the other rivers in Florida.

Some of the history of steamboats on the Suwannee River was detailed in chapter 1 and as noted before, accounts of activity on this river are very sketchy. A recent discovery of a paper from the Florida Historical Society by Edward A. Mueller has given us a little more information. The paper was written in January of 1967 and printed in the *Historical Quarterly* in volume 45, issue 3. Details are found in the bibliography at the end of the book.

According to Mueller, Suwannee was spelled with only one "n" around the time of the Civil War. He mentions the *Minerva* and the *Izard* as government-chartered steamboats used to transport supplies to the outposts on the Suwannee during the Second Seminole Indian War.

The river was made better for navigation by a suggested improvement to clear the oyster bars at the mouth in 1839. A nine-foot channel was suggested and probably undertaken because in 1845 the river was being used by at least one steamboat (Mueller, East Coast, 242).

In 1845, the government contemplated establishing a mail route by steamers on the Suwannee from Cedar Key to Fort White to be connected by stage coach with the St. Johns. The steamboat *Orpheus* was built in New Orleans especially for that purpose. She was 136 feet long and had eighteen staterooms. She would carry the mail from Cedar Key to the new town of Santa Fe on the Santa Fe River, in Columbia County, once a week. She would also run the Suwannee to the flourishing town of Columbus (*St. Augustine News*, October 25, 1845).

According to *Lytle's Merchant Steam Vessels of the United States*, the *Orpheus* was actually built in Pittsburgh, Pennsylvania, in 1841, and three years later registered at St. Marks, Florida, near the Suwannee. She remained in operation until 1847 and met her end in some manner on the Suwannee (Lytle).

The next steamboat on the Suwannee after the *Orpheus* appears to be the *Glasgow*. This boat was originally from Louisville, Kentucky, but was enrolled in St. Marks from 1849 to 1851 and possibly for a longer time. During the latter part of her enrollment, she served on the Suwannee. The exact nature of her operations is unknown. The records show the boat was 49 tons gross, having one deck and a square stern. She was 100 feet long and 19 feet wide with a draft of 2 feet, 9 inches. The shallow draft made the boat very suitable for the shallow reaches of the river. David Bell was the *Glasgow*'s master and part owner (Lytle).

During the Civil War, steamboat activity on the Suwannee was brought almost to a standstill. The first Federal naval raid in Florida was against Cedar Key. The town was the terminus of the Florida Railroad and was also known as the center of blockade running. A landing party from the *U.S.S. Hatteras* descended on the town on January 16, 1862, and destroyed the railroad depot and wharf, seven freight cars, the telegraph office, warehouses, three sloops, four schooners, and a ferry barge. Steamboat operations on the Suwannee were impossible after the fall of Cedar Key because the Federal blockaders now had control of the nearby Suwannee (Mueller, *Suwannee River*, 8).

After the Civil War the *Wawenock* was the first known steamer to operate on the river. She was built in Wiscasset, Maine, in November 1863 and used by the United States government during the war. From 1865 to 1868, the boat operated out of Norfolk, Virginia. The *Wawenock* was 109 feet long by 19 feet wide with a draft of 4.5 feet and in 1868 was enlarged to be 128 feet long by 27 feet wide with a 5-foot draft. This brought the vessel to a capacity of 128 tons gross. The boat ran from Cedar Key to New Troy on the Suwannee River in 1872. She connected on a once-a-week basis at Cedar Key with vessels plying the Gulf between Key West and New Orleans. The *Wawenock* served on the Suwannee until late in the summer of 1874 and was moved to Pensacola in the same year. She finally ceased operations and was broken up in New Orleans in 1880 (278).

After the *Wawenock*, the next vessel to serve on the Suwannee was probably the *Erie*. This boat was 70 feet long by 21 feet wide with a draft of 4.3 feet. She had a plain head and a round stern. The vessel came to Cedar Key sometime in the summer of 1880 and was owned by various merchants along the river. The boat was basically a freighter but carried passengers on occasion. In 1883, the *Erie* was sold to investors in Manatee County (279).

In the 1880s as the railroads began to cross the state, it appeared that the steamboats and the railroads would complement each other, but that wasn't always the case. Henry B. Plant played a significant role in the history of steamboats on the Suwannee. The railroad man used the steamers on several rivers to help construct the railroad and to fill in the missing links for transportation until the lines could be completed.

Plant began using the *Caddo Belle* on the Suwannee in July of 1883 and continued until the fall of 1885. The *Caddo Belle* was never very successful. She was built in Portsmouth, Ohio, in 1880 and was operated out of New Orleans until 1881. The boat was then transferred to the Apalachicola River and finally to the Suwannee.

The *Caddo Belle* was of 167 tons and was 125 feet long by 25 feet wide with a draft of 3.5 feet. The boat had two decks and was a stern-wheeler. She carried passengers on her top deck and freight on the lower to connect to the railroad at Branford, Florida.

The *Eva* was another vessel that operated on the Suwannee. She was 100 feet long by 22 feet wide with a 3-foot draft. She was of 115 tons. The *Eva* was built in New Orleans with a plain head and square stern and was in service until April 1883, when she was wrecked and sunk.

The owner of *Eva* was John Miller of Tampa who owned several vessels that ran from Tampa to Gulf ports like Cedar Key. The *Eva* was not described as a boat that would be used on the open Gulf but probably was in fair weather (Mueller, *Suwannee River*, 279).

Robert Absalom Ivey came to Florida as a youth and was born in Baldwin County, Georgia, in 1840. He was in the Confederate Army at age sixteen as a water boy and lived through several engagements. After the war, Ivey and his two brothers, Jess and F. C., moved to Branford. Branford was never a very large community, but it became the upstream capital of the Suwannee River. Much of its growth and progress was due to Captain Bob Ivey.

Ivey was a friend of George F. Drew, who served as governor of Florida from 1877 to 1881. Drew owned a sawmill and some valuable naval stores operations in Branford, and he and Ivey shared similar interests.

Ivey's first steamboat was the *Suwanee*. The boat's name was spelled with only one "n" throughout her life. The *Suwanee* was a 51-ton vessel, 70 feet long by 16.5 feet wide with a draft of 4 feet. It is believed that her engines came from the *Susie B.* which was built at Middleport, Ohio. The *Susie B.* was originally named the *St. Jacobs Oil* by the Baltimore drug firm that owned her. In March of 1883, she was sold to the New Orleans Times Democrat Publishing Company and her name was changed to *Susie B.* The steamer was used around the Cedar Key area until 1887 when Captain T.

A. Wallace bought her for the cedar towing business in the Gulf and on the Withlacoochee River. He owned the boat until December of 1888 when according to the records she was wrecked by her owner. In the following year Captain Ivey utilized the engines in the *Suwanee* when she was first documented in 1889 (282).

In September of 1889, the *Suwanee* was sold to E. W. Prince of Carlson, Florida, and he ran the vessel on the Withlacoochee River until August of 1898. The *Suwanee* was used on the Caloosahatchee River by Conrad and Fred Menge to run between Ft. Myers and Lake Okeechobee. In the 1920s, the *Suwanee* sank near Moore Haven, Florida.

Captain Ivey built a dredge for the U.S. Army Corps of Engineers in 1889. It was also named the *Suwanee*. The dredge was a stern-wheeler of 95 tons, 100 feet long by 24 feet wide with a draft of 4 feet. She was used on the Suwannee to clear snags and to do dredging. The vessel would later be used on the Ocklawaha River and others until 1911. She was sold to the Hillsborough Dredging Company of Tampa, and her name changed to the *Dredge Hester*. She remained in service until July 23, 1911, when she burned at the Narrows south of Indian Rock in Tampa Bay (283).

After the *Dredge Hester*, Captain Ivey built the most famous and celebrated steamboat ever to travel the Suwannee River. She was the *Belle of the Suwannee* and was completed in 1889. The boat was 180 tons with a length of 111 feet by 24 feet wide with a draft of 4 feet. The *Belle* was a typical two-decked stern-wheeler and was named after Ivey's daughter, Bertha. Bertha christened the *Belle* at her launching and thus began the saga of the *Belle of the Suwannee*, a "legend in her own time." One reason for her fame was the bridal chambers that Ivey installed aboard. The Suwannee River had become a place for newlyweds to vacation, and the chambers on the *Belle* were used quite frequently (Mueller, *Suwannee River*, 284).

Sometime in 1893 the *Sam Pyles* appeared on the Suwannee. The *Sam Pyles* was built at Panasoffkee, Florida, in 1885 with two decks and a stern wheel and was owned by the Plant Investment Company. The boat was 76 feet long by 17 feet wide with a draft of 3.7 feet; she was able to carry very few passengers because of her small size. The boat was named after her first owner, Samuel R. Pyles, of Panasoffkee, who was also her skipper until she was sold to the Plant Company in December of 1892. The boat had also run on the Withlacoochee River and Lakes Apopka, Tsala, and Panasoffkee.

21. The *Belle of the Suwannee* was one of the most popular boats on the river. Photo used by permission of the Florida Photographic Archives.

The South Florida and Western Railroad Company purchased the *Sam Pyles* in May of 1899 and operated her for four years. The boat was sold to a naval stores concern in Savannah, Georgia, but there are no records of her after 1909.

The *Louisa* was transferred to the Suwannee from her service on coastal Georgia rivers in 1894. She was built at Dublin, Georgia, in 1890 and was 101 feet long by 25 feet wide with a draft of 5 feet. The vessel was of 200 net tons and owned by Captain E. L. Magruder, who in addition to his Suwannee River activities was an owner and master on the Chattahoochee and Apalachicola river systems for many years. He lived in Apalachicola much of the time.

The *Louisa* was a challenge to Robert Ivey's *Belle of the Suwannee,* so Ivey constructed his largest vessel, the *C. D. Owens,* to meet the competition. The *Owens* was 135 feet long by 33 feet wide with a draft of 4.8 feet and named for an official of the Savannah, Florida, and Western Railroad who was Ivey's friend. The boat was owned by Ivey and the Suwannee River Steamboat Company. It ended up in the hands of the Independent Navigation Company on the Apalachicola River until March 21, 1899, when it was destroyed by fire at Columbus, Georgia.

Sometime in 1898, Captain Robert Ivey bought the *C. U. Sheppherd.* This boat had been used on the Withlacoochee River to haul phosphate and was a shallow water tug type of a vessel. She was built in Jacksonville in 1892 and was 52 feet long by 18 feet wide with a draft of 3.3 feet. The Suwannee River Steamboat Company bought her from Ivey in 1901. By 1904, she was listed as inactive.

After 1896, steamboating on the Suwannee River was past its prime years. The Independent Navigation Company, which was owned by Captain E. L. Magruder, made one last fling with Suwannee River service by bringing in the *Thetis* from Apalachicola. This boat was of 61 tons and 97 feet long by 19.5 feet wide with a draft of 3.8 feet.

A few months after the *Thetis* arrived, the Gulf Transportation Company brought in the *City of Hawkinsville.* She was one of the largest boats ever to operate on the river being 141 feet long by 31 feet wide with a draft of 5.7 feet. This vessel was built in Abbeville, Georgia, in 1896 and was first used between Hawkinsville and Darien, Georgia, on the Altamaha River (285–287).

In the summer of 1900, she came to Florida and ran here until May 19, 1922, when she was stripped of her machinery and abandoned by her last captain, M. Currie. Today the *Hawkinsville* is an underwater archaeological preserve that can be seen where she was abandoned just south of the old railroad trestle near Old Town, Florida. The *Hawkinsville* was the last of the steamboats that operated on the Suwannee. If you are a diver, it is useful to know that the old vessel is located in shallow water and is an approved dive site by the state of Florida. More information can be found on the Internet about the *Hawkinsville.*

On a map in 1544 the Spanish called the Peace River "Rio de la Paz," or river of peace, and the Seminoles called it "Tallackchopo," or cow peas. The river originates either in Polk County's Green Swamp or, as some say, in

Lake Hancock near Lakeland. At any rate, it winds beautifully and peacefully for around 105 miles from its source to Charlotte Harbor at Punta Gorda. It is quite an unlikely place to find a steamboat, especially as far north from Port Charlotte as Ft. Meade. The river is wide and deep at Port Charlotte, but by the time it reaches Ft. Meade, it has a lot of very shallow water along with a variety of snags and obstructions on the bottom. In the 1800s, it must have been a nightmare to navigate.

Most of the information about a steamboat on the Peace River in Ft. Meade was given to me by a fellow historian, Lloyd Harris of Bartow, Florida. When he found out I was doing a book about steamboats, he told me of an article he had done for his radio show *Imperial Moments* called "Steamboat a'Comin.'" Lloyd had the radio show for awhile on a local station, and the subjects for the show were historical events that happened in Polk County. Lloyd said Captain Benjamin Franklin Hall was the master of the boat, and the boat was called the "*Schipman*." Further, there was a picture of the boat sitting by the bridge in Ft. Meade in the Florida State Archives. The boat wasn't listed in the steamboat section of the archives, but it is recorded under bridges. The story sounded too far-fetched to be true, so I checked it out and found that he was right.

In 1887, the South Florida Railroad circulated pamphlets advertising the Central Florida towns of Winter Haven, Auburndale, Bartow, Lakeland, and Fort Meade, hoping to induce people to come to these places. Just south of Bartow was a beautiful artesian spring called Kissengen Springs that was promoted on a full-color lithograph print replete with boaters and bathhouses. It was a recreational paradise, with crystal-clear water in a natural setting—a place everyone hoped rich Northerners would come to go swimming.

The upper portion of the advertisement displayed a trolley car with side panels, a painted steam car, Bartow, and in the lower portion, the Peace River with a steamboat.

The trolley car line existed only as an unfulfilled dream, but the steamboat came nearer to fruition. Captain Benjamin Franklin Hall, of Kissimmee River fame, purchased a boat called the *Schipman* that was built in Chicago and was a 35-foot side-wheel vessel. The boat was shipped to Kissimmee by rail and had a small cabin with forward and rear covered decks. Two masts sported U.S. flags. There was also a small smokestack. An anchor on the bow completed the picture of this versatile boat. Hall and his son owned a number of boats in the Kissimmee area and were best known for the *Bertha Lee* that he took across the Gulf, up the Caloosahatchee, across Lake Okeechobee, and up the Kissimmee River. It took him fifty-one days to make the trip from Lake Okeechobee to Kissimmee because the boat was bigger than the river. The story of the *Bertha Lee* and the Halls is in chapter 3 of this book.

On July 13, 1887, the *Bartow Advance-Courier* newspaper reported,

> Captain Hall, having successfully reached Ft. Meade with his steamboat *Shipman*, proceeded at once to Kissengen Springs with a civil engineer and examined the channel. After careful sounding and checking up of the obstructions (fallen timbers, brush and drift) he came to the conclusion that he could force his boat up to the mouth of the springs after a little work had been done. The citizens of Ft. Meade are now assisting in this preliminary opening of a channel and hope to soon have a new route of access to this pleasant resort. The above is from a gentleman of Ft. Meade, and we insert it with the additional remarks that the Springs has long been known, and that by running a regular line from Bartow by land, visitors will be able to have, in addition to this natural phenomenon, the pleasures (rare enough in these parts) of a boat ride through a very picturesque portion of Peace River. It is hoped that Bartow will not be behind her sister town in aiding to establish an open channel.

Two weeks later, citizens of Ft. Meade bought a controlling interest in the steamboat venture and began clearing logs. Six months later, and only three miles north of Ft. Meade, Captain Hall turned his steamboat south and headed back to the brown waters of the Kissimmee River. Steamboating on the northern reaches of the Peace River had ended in failure (Harris).

As far as we know, no other steamboat ever traveled on the Peace River as far north as Ft. Meade. There was one steamer called the *Peter Raulerson* that made regular trips as far north as Fort Ogden where alligator hides were loaded for shipment to northern points (Covington, 184–185).

In 1857 to 1871, there were numerous small settlements along the coastline of west Florida from above Tampa Bay to below Charlotte Harbor. Their only means of communication was by the Gulf of Mexico and river steamboats. Some of these towns had only one municipal dock, while in others there were various public or private docks along the way. A list of these little settlements includes Bayport, Anclote River, Clearwater Harbor, Law's Store, McMullen's Store, Phillippi's Grove, Point Pinellas, Alafia, Terraceia Bay, Little Manatee, Manatee, Sarasota, Charlotte Harbor, and Punta Rassa. Even with the steamboats, transportation and mail service was bad for many years until roads could be built and the railroads finally came. The steamboats were familiar sights along the west coast, and one stern-wheeler, the *Gopher*, operated as far up the Hillsborough River as Sulphur Springs and along the Alafia to Riverview. Various passenger and freight boats made their way between points of Tampa Bay, including Tampa, St. Petersburg, and Sarasota. A line consisting of two steamers carried mail and passengers up the Little Manatee River to Ellenton and Palmetto.

Because of the shallow waters, navigation in Tampa Bay was very difficult until a channel was dredged. One boat captain had posts erected at various points to mark the six- to fifteen-foot natural channel that meandered along the western shore of the bay. At night he had oil-burning lanterns placed on the posts, but sometimes log rafts on their way to the sawmills would hit the posts and destroy them. This caused many boats to miss the channel (162–184).

Excursion boats operated along the coast and brought relaxation to the people. Picnic trips were taken to islands lying near the mainland. Sometimes two excursion vessels leaving the same dock would engage in a race, much to the delight of the passengers. The most popular excursion trip was from Tampa to Bradenton, with stops at St. Petersburg, Manatee, and Palmetto (185).

For many years, the only way to go from Tampa to St. Petersburg was by steamboat. In 1910 three steamers operating on Tampa Bay were owned by the H. Walter Fuller Investment Company. They were the *Favorite, H. B. Plant,* and the *Manatee*. These vessels operated between Tampa, Bradenton, and Sarasota, with a stop at the Electric Pier in St. Petersburg. This Electric Pier stood a little to the south of the present location of the municipal or "Million Dollar" pier, and streetcars ran very close to the pier's edge.

Pass-a-Grille beach was a magnet for tourists and residents who wished to enjoy a beautiful beach and friendly waters. Since Pass-a-Grille was not connected to the mainland by bridges at that time, the only way to get

22. An old postcard shows the Manatee River Fleet near Bradenton. Photo used by permission of the Florida Photographic Archives.

to it was by boat. People from Tampa frequently took the three-hour trip across the bay to the friendly island (Covington, 381). There were only two ways to travel the west coast of Florida in the 1865 to 1884 period. One method was to go by railroad to Cedar Key and then take a boat to a seacoast town.

Miller, Henderson, and Company owned the Tampa Steamship Company, and their vessel, the *T. J. Cochran,* ran between Cedar Key and Tampa, touching at all Manatee River landings. This boat made the trip to and from Cedar Key all week, and every Tuesday and Friday made a connection at Tampa with the Tampa and Key West Steamship Company's steamer *Dictator* for Key West and Punta Rassa. Another company, the Gulf Steamship Company, ran the *Governor Stafford* along the coast from Tampa to Cedar Key. It was a $30,000 vessel built by the Pusey and Jones Company of Wilmington, Delaware. The ship was 130 feet long with a draft of only 3.5 feet, making her very suitable for shallow water. The boat was fitted out with first-class accommodations for passengers.

The Plant Investment Company ran a line of steamers from Tampa to Key West and Havana. A connection was made at Tampa with the South

23. Steamboats like the *F. S. Lewis* were used on Alachua Lake near Gainesville in the 1880s. Photo used by permission of the Florida Photographic Archives.

Florida Railroad. A smaller boat went along the coast to the shallow water harbors as far as Manatee (377).

The Kinzie Brothers' steamship line traveled from Ft. Myers to Sanibel, Pine Island, and Captiva. A steamship line owned by the Menge Brothers operated on the Caloosahatchee River between Ft. Myers and LaBelle. The Miller and Henderson Company, which later became the Tampa Steamship Company, was the largest shipping company in southern Florida. It controlled many vessels including the *Lizzie Henderson, Captain Miller, Alabama, T. J. Cochran, Hosteher, Eliza Hancox,* and *Lucy Miller.* The *Lizzie Henderson* and *Lucy Miller* were vessels specially built to carry bananas from Panama to Tampa (380).

A very unusual place to find steamboats in Florida was in Alachua County, where Gainesville is located. Commerce and travel was depen-

24. The *Alert* carried tourists and fruit from the railhead at Waldo down the Waldo Canal in the 1870s. The canal was twelve miles long and ran between lakes Alto and Santa Fe. Photo used by permission of the Florida Photographic Archives.

dent on steamboats before the road system and gasoline-powered vehicles appeared. One of the best-known steamers was the *F. S. Lewis*, a two-decked paddle wheeler. This boat served Gainesville and its agricultural area in the 1880s on Alachua Lake. Paynes Prairie is a well-known stretch of land that interstate 75 crosses on its way to Gainesville. Today, there is not much water there unless the area is subjected to heavy rains. In 1871, the rains came and by 1873 Paynes Prairie had become Alachua Lake. Alachua Sink, which is part of the prairie, had become clogged, and the lake formed because there was no drain for the area. The steamboats ran here until the Alachua Sink became unclogged in 1892.

The boats were important for a longer period of time after the lake disappeared. They connected the rail terminal at Waldo via the Waldo Canal that was dug in the 1870s. This canal connected Lake Alto and Lake Santa

Fe, and the boats were turned into pleasure vessels filled with tourists when they were not being used for commerce.

Steamboats operated in many other places in Florida, and there were many other boats not mentioned in this book. The story of the steamboat in our state is fading into obscurity but needs to be known because the boats had such an economic and physical impact in the development of not just Florida but the whole country. The men who built and operated the boats were true pioneers who should be remembered for their contributions.

Acknowledgments

I want to acknowledge all of my friends and relatives who stood by me during the process of writing this book. Without their help, it would have been impossible.

A special thank you goes to Joyce Sanborn who did the proofreading and to my wife Linda who supports me in all my efforts.

Thanks also to Timothy O'Keefe, who brought the manuscript to the attention of the University Press of Florida, and to John Byram, my editor, for being there from the beginning to help.

Bibliography

American Guide Series. *A Guide to the Southernmost State.* New York: Oxford University Press, 1939.

Answers.com. "Jacksonville. History, Winter Resort Era." http://answers.com/topic/jacksonville-florida.html, accessed May 20, 2005.

Apalachicola and Chattahoochee Rivers. "Cruising America's Waterways." http://members.aol.com/americacruising/appalachicola-chattahoochee.html, accessed June 24, 2005.

Bair, Cinnamon. "Fax Philly Failed in Florida." *Lakeland Ledger,* 2005.

Bartow Advance Courier Newspaper, July 1887.

BootsnAll Travel. "Gulfport, Florida: A Gem of a Town." http://bootsnall.com/articles/00-07/gulfport-florida-a-gem-of-a-town-florida-usa.html, accessed July 8, 2005.

Burnett, Gene. "The Suwannee: Meandering through Florida History." *Florida Trend Magazine,* June 1986.

Cantrell, Elizabeth A. *When Kissimmee Was Young.* Kissimmee, Fla.: Osceola County Historical Society, 1948.

Carr, Archie. "All the Way Down Upon the Suwannee." Suwannee County Centennial, September 28–October 4, 1958. Live Oak, Fla.

Covington, James W. *The Story of Southwest Florida.* New York: Lewis Historical Publishing Company, 1957.

Exploring Florida. "The Suwannee River." http://fcit.usf.edu/florida/lessons/suwannee/suwannee.htm, accessed May 17, 2005.

Florida's Underwater Archaeological Preserves "City of Hawkinsville," http://www.flheritage.com/archaeology/underwater/preserve/uwcity.cfm, accessed June 17, 2005.

"*Floridelphia* Polk County, Florida." http://diglib.lib.fsu.edu/cgi-bin/ebind2html.pl/fs00000072?seq=1, accessed August 9, 2005.

Franklin County History. "Chapter 7. Apalachicola, Welcome to Highway 98." http://www.ushighway98.com/Apalachicola-history.htm, accessed May 17, 2005.

Harner, Charles E. *Florida's Promoters*. Tampa: Trend Publications, 1973.

Harris, Lloyd, "Steamboat A'Comin'," July 23, 2001. WBAR radio, *Imperial Moments*, Bartow, Fla.

Hetherington, Alma. *The River of the Long Water*. St. Petersburg, Fla.: Southern Heritage Press, 1980.

Historic North Brevard Florida. http://www.nbbd.com/godo/history/landmarks/01.html, accessed January 30, 2006.

History for Fanning Springs State Park. "Fanning Springs State Park History." http://www.floridastateparks.org/fanningsprings/History.cfm, accessed July 6, 2005.

Hopwood, Fred A. *The Golden Era of Steamboating on the Indian River 1877–1900*. Cocoa, Fla.: Florida Historical Society Press, 1998.

Iatarola, Louis M. Profile in Tacony History. "Volume 8: The Life and Influence of Hamilton Disston." http://members.aol.com/historictacony2/profile_hamilton.html, accessed September 23, 2005.

Indian River Historical Cruise. http://www.nbbd.com/HistoricalCruise/index.html, accessed January 12, 2006.

Kaucher, Dorothy. *The Suwannee*. Orlando, Fla.: Kirstein and Sons Printers, 1972.

Keaton, Richard, and Sharyn Kane. "Chapter 15: Hard Times," http://www.cr.nps.gov/seac/benning-book/ch15.htm, accessed May 17, 2005.

Kissimmee River Restoration History. http://www.sfwmd.gov/org/erd/krr/pastpres/krrhisto.html, accessed July 7, 2005.

Lytle, William M. *Merchant Steam Vessels of the United States 1807–1868*. Mystic, Conn.: Steamship Historical Society of America, 1952.

Mitchell, C. Bradford. "Paddle-Wheel Inboard: Some of the History of the Ocklawaha River Steamboating and of the Hart Line." *The American Neptune*, Salem, Mass., April–July 1947.

Mueller, Edward A. "East Coast Florida Steamboating 1831–1861." *Florida Historical Quarterly*, Vol. 30, January 1962.

———. *Ocklawaha River Steamboats*. Jacksonville: Mendelson Printing Company, 1983.

———. *Perilous Journeys: A History of Steamboating on the Chattahoochee, Apalachicola, and Flint Rivers, 1828–1928*. Eufaula, Ala.: Historic Chattahoochee Commission, 1990.

———. *Steamboating on the St. Johns 1830–1885*. Melbourne, Fla.: Kellersberger Fund of the South Brevard Historical Society, 1984.

———. *St. Johns River Steamboats*. Published by the author. 1986.

———. "Suwannee River Steamboating." *Florida Historical Quarterly*, Vol. 45, No. 3, January 1967.

Osceola County Centennial: 1887–1987. Kissimmee, Fla.: Cody Publications, 1987.

Proctor, Samuel. *Napoleon Bonaparte Broward, Florida's Fighting Democrat.* Gainesville, Fla.: University Press of Florida, 1950.

Restoring the Ocklawaha River Ecosystem. http://www.fldfenders.org/publications/restoring1.html, accessed October 2, 2005.

Runnymede-Ghosttown. http://www.ghosttowns.com/states/fl/runnymede.html, accessed July 20, 2005.

St. Augustine News, October 25, 1845. Unknown writer.

Tebeau, Charlton W. *A History of Florida.* Miami: University of Miami Press, 1971.

Towart, James W. "The Maple Leaf in Historical Perspective." http://mapleleafshipwreck.com/Book/introduction/intro1.htm, accessed June 27, 2005.

U.S. Snagboat *Montgomery*: A National Historic Landmark. "A Brief History of Steam-Powered River Transportation and of the U.S. Snagboat *Montgomery.*" http://montgomery.sam.usace.army.mil/about.html, accessed May 17, 2005.

Will, Lawrence E. *Cracker History of Okeechobee.* St. Petersburg, Fla.: Great Outdoors Publishers, 1964.

Index

Page numbers in italics refer to illustrations.

Bob Bass is a freelance writer and photographer whose work has appeared in *Florida Living, Florida Wildlife, Lost Treasure, Living Aboard,* and many other national magazines. He has served on the board of directors for the Florida Outdoor Writers Association and is an active member. His Web site is southernfreestyle.com.